THE
LITTLE GIANT® BOOK
OF
FOOTBALL
FACTS

THE
LITTLE GIANT® BOOK
OF
FOOTBALL
FACTS

MICHAEL J. PELLOWSKI

Sterling Publishing Co., Inc.
New York

TO PETER & JOYCE HENDRICKS

Library of Congress Cataloging-in-Publication Data

Pellowski, Michael.
  Little giant book of football facts / Michael J. Pellowski.
      p. cm.
  Includes index.
  ISBN 1-4027-2390-3
  1. Football—Miscellanea—Juvenile literature. I. Title.
GV950.7.P45 2005
796.332'64'0973—dc22

                                    2005001146

10   9   8   7   6   5   4   3   2   1

Published by Sterling Publishing Co., Inc.
387 Park Avenue South, New York, NY 10016
© 2005 by Michael Pellowski
Distributed in Canada by Sterling Publishing
c/o Canadian Manda Group, 165 Dufferin Street
Toronto, Ontario, Canada M6K 3H6
Distributed in Great Britain and Europe by Chris Lloyd at Orca Book
Services, Stanley House, Fleets Lane, Poole BH15 3AJ, England
Distributed in Australia by Capricorn Link (Australia) Pty. Ltd.
P.O. Box 704, Windsor, NSW 2756, Australia

Sterling ISBN 1-4027-2390-3

For information about custom editions, special sales, premium and
corporate purchases, please contact Sterling Special Sales
Department at 800-805-5489 or specialsales@sterlingpub.com.

CONTENTS

A veteran quarterback quickly studies the alignment of the defense across the line of scrimmage as he walks up behind his massive, offensive linemen. The QB then crouches behind his burly center and loudly barks signals to his teammates.

"Blue. Eighty-two! Blue. Eighty-two. Hut! Hut! Hut!" The center snaps the ball through his legs and into the palms of the signal caller. The QB hands the pigskin to a speedy back who veers off the crushing blocks of his guard and tackle.

Wham! A big, tough linebacker meets the running back head on and tackles him to the turf for no gain.

This is the game of football! For over one hundred and thirty years, this rough and tumble American sport has excited, thrilled and electrified coaches, players, and fans alike.

In this book, you'll find over 1,000 interesting and odd football facts and feats. You'll meet gridiron greats from the college and pro ranks. You'll learn about terrific teams and super Super Bowl moments. You'll marvel at fantastic football records and giggle at goofy gridiron mishaps. It's all here in these pages from crunching quarterback sacks to dazzling touchdown dashes.

So, huddle up with some sport friends or sit down alone and enjoy a fact-packed book all about one of the world's most popular hard-hitting games. Turn these pages if you're ready for some football fun.

CHAPTER 1

FIRST & GO!

Being first is important in any sport. Being the first person or team to accomplish a specific feat is a unique achievement. In football, there are many historic and record-setting firsts which have contributed to making both college and pro football the popular games they are today.

Find out about the first football helmets worn by players. Learn who scored the first touchdown in Super Bowl history. Discover when the first All-American team was selected. Have fun as you gain a ton of gridiron knowledge reading about these and other amazing football firsts.

The term "football" was first used in Britain during the Middle Ages as another name for soccer.

■

The first football games played in America were variations of the game of soccer. Carrying or throwing the ball was not permitted.

The balls used for the first American football games were made of inflated pig bladders, which is how a football became known as a pigskin.

■

The first football games in America were played with teams made up of 25 players on each side. That meant there were 50 players involved in the game all at one time.

■

The first football helmets came into use in the early 1890's. They were made of leather with flaps that covered players' ears.

Early football helmets had no face masks. Some players in the 1890's wore a hollow metal device which resembled a shoehorn over their noses for protection. The nose guard was held in place by straps.

■

The first football uniforms appeared in 1877. The uniforms were designed by a Princeton University footballer named L.P. Smock. Each uniform consisted of a canvas jacket, black knee pants, stockings, and a black jersey trimmed in orange (black and orange are Princeton's team colors).

■

Shoulder pads first became part of a football player's regular equipment in the mid-1920's.

■

It was in the mid-1920's that football players first began to use knee pads, hip pads, thigh pads, and spiked shoes.

Improved football helmets made of plastic first came into use in the mid-1940's after the end of World War II.

∎

The man credited with placing the first face bars on football helmets was professional football coach Paul Brown of the Cleveland Browns.

The color of the first NFL penalty flags was white. In 1965, the National Football League Rules Committee changed the color of penalty flags from white to yellow.

■

The first college football game was played on a field measuring 120 yards long and 75 yards wide. It took place on November 6, 1869 in New Brunswick, New Jersey. Students from Rutgers, the State University of New Jersey, played students from Princeton University on the Rutgers' campus. Rutgers won, beating Princeton six goals to four.

■

There were no touchdowns tallied in college football's first game. A ball kicked through a goal 24 feet wide counted as a single point or goal.

■

The first college football captains for an official game were William S. Gummere of Princeton University and William T. Legget of Rutgers University. The captains met on the field of play on November 6, 1869.

The first interstate college football game in history took place in 1870. Rutgers University of New Jersey played Columbia University of New York. Rutgers defeated Columbia six goals to two in the contest.

■

Harvard played Yale in football for the first time in 1875. Harvard won the game four to zero.

Harvard University formed its first football squad in 1871.

■

Yale University formed its first football team in 1872.

■

Cornell University formed its first football squad in 1873.

■

The first college football All-American team was picked in 1889. The squad was selected by Caspar Whitney and Walter Camp, early pioneers and promoters of the sport.

■

Walter Camp, a football player for Yale in the early 1880's, helped establish many of football's first rules and regulations. It was Camp's idea to start play from a line of scrimmage. It was his idea to have eleven players on a side. Walter Camp also came up with the concept of having a system of "downs" to advance the ball.

Yale teammates Amos Alonzo Stagg and William "Pudge" Heffelfinger were members of the very first All-American football team. Stagg was an end on the 1889 team and Heffelfinger was a guard. Both men later played key roles in the development of football.

■

Amos Alonzo Stagg, who coached at the University of Chicago, College of the Pacific, and Susquehanna University, was the first football coach to use tackling dummies and blocking sleds. He was also the inventor of the onside kick and men in motion.

■

William "Pudge" Heffelfinger is believed to be football's first paid player. In 1892, Heffelfinger is alleged to have received five hundred dollars to play in a football game between two athletic clubs in Pittsburgh, Pennsylvania.

Football teams used verbal signals and set plays for the first time in 1882.

■

The University of Georgia was the first football team to use a huddle. In 1896, Georgia huddled up in a game against Auburn.

1. Who was the first NFL football player named the Associated Press Athlete of the Year? Here are some hints. He was 43-years-old when he won the award in 1970.

■

2. Who was the first player selected in the 2004 NFL draft?

■

3. Chuck Howley was the first player who was not a quarterback to be named MVP of a Super Bowl. What position did Chuck Howley play?

■

4. A quarterback won the Heisman Trophy (given to college football's top player) for the first time in 1938. A famous football award is now named after that winner. Who is he?

Answers

1. The first NFL football player to be named the A.P. Athlete of the Year was quarterback and place-kicker George Blanda of the Oakland Raiders. Blanda, who was 43 years old at the time, took over for injured Q.B. Daryle Lamonica and led the Raiders to the AFC Western Division Championship.

2. Quarterback Eli Manning was the first college football player selected in the 2004 NFL Draft.

3. Chuck Howley was a linebacker for the Dallas Cowboys, who won Super Bowl V in 1971 by beating the Baltimore Colts 16 to 13.

4. In 1938, Davey O'Brien of Texas Christian University became the first quarterback to win the Heisman Trophy. The Davey O'Brien Trophy has been awarded to the top college quarterback in America since 1981.

The first player from the University of Notre Dame to win the Heisman Trophy was quarterback Angelo Bertelli. Bertelli was named college football's top player in 1943.

■

Yale University was the first Ivy League school to defeat the University of Notre Dame in football. In 1914, Yale beat Notre Dame 28 to 0 on the gridiron.

The University of Notre Dame earned its first gridiron victory in a major bowl contest in 1925. Notre Dame defeated Stanford in the 1925 Rose Bowl by the score of 27 to 10.

■

The University of Michigan beat Stanford University 49 to 0 in the first Rose Bowl game, which was played in 1902.

■

In 1935, Tulane beat Temple 20 to 14 in the first Sugar Bowl football contest.

■

The University of Miami (Florida) defeated Manhattan College 7 to 0 in the first Orange Bowl game, which was played in 1933.

■

Texas Christian University topped Marquette University by the score of 16 to 6 in the first Cotton Bowl Football Classic, which was held in 1937.

The winner of the first Gator Bowl football game was Wake Forest. In 1946, Wake Forest beat South Carolina 26 to 14 in the Gator Bowl.

■

The first Liberty Bowl game was held in 1959. Penn State outscored Alabama 7 to 0 to win the first Liberty Bowl.

■

Lionel Taylor of the Denver Broncos was the first player in the AFL or NFL to catch 100 passes in a single season. Taylor made 100 catches in 1961.

The NFL was first known as the American Professional Football Association (APFA). The APFA changed its name to the National Football League in 1922.

■

The Akron (Ohio) Pros were the first champions of the American Professional Football Association. The Akron Pros were crowned champions of the APFA in 1920, when the league title went to the team with the best regular season record.

The first NFL Championship playoff game was held in 1932 when the Chicago Bears and the Portsmouth (Ohio) Spartans ended the 1932 regular season with identical records. The Bears beat the Spartans 9 to 0 to capture the NFL crown.

■

Halfback Barry Sanders of the Detroit Lions was the first pro football player to rush for 1,000 yards in each of his first ten pro seasons.

The NFL's first indoor championship game was December 18, 1932. The championship playoff game between the Chicago Bears and the Portsmouth Spartans was scheduled to be played outdoors at Wrigley Field that year. A snowstorm forced the 1932 championship to be held indoors in Chicago Stadium instead.

■

Walter Payton of the Chicago Bears led the league in kickoff returns in 1975, in his first year in the National Football League. He averaged 31.7 yards per return.

■

The first New York Giants back to gain over 200 yards in a single game was Gene Roberts. Roberts rushed for 218 yards on 26 carries against the Chicago Cardinals on November 12, 1950.

SUPER (BOWL) FIRSTS

At the start of training camp, all professional football teams have one goal in mind: To make the Super Bowl. Let's see how many of the following Super Bowl firsts you know.

■

The first Super Bowl contest matched the Green Bay Packers of the NFL against the Kansas City Chiefs of the AFL. The game was played on January 15, 1967 at the Memorial Coliseum in Los Angeles, California. Green Bay beat Kansas City 35 to 10.

■

Receiver Max McGee of the Green Bay Packers scored the first touchdown in Super Bowl history. McGee caught a 37-yard touchdown pass from quarterback Bart Starr in the first quarter of Super Bowl I.

■

Hank Stram, of the Kansas City Chiefs, was the first coach to lose a Super Bowl game.

Quarterback Bart Starr, of the Green Bay Packers, was the first Super Bowl MVP. Starr connected on 17 of 23 passes for 250 yards and 2 touchdowns in the contest.

■

Vince Lombardi, of the Green Bay Packers, was the first football coach to win a Super Bowl championship.

■

Fullback Jim Taylor of the Green Bay Packers scored the first rushing touchdown in Super Bowl history. Taylor had a 14-yard T.D. run in the second quarter of Super Bowl I.

■

The first player to score three touchdowns in a single Super Bowl game was running back Roger Craig of the San Francisco 49ers. Craig rushed for one touchdown and caught two T.D. passes against the Miami Dolphins in the 1985 Super Bowl (XIX).

AFRICAN-AMERICAN FIRSTS

Ernie Davis of Syracuse University was the first African-American football player to win the Heisman Trophy, which is awarded annually to college football's top player. Davis, a running back, won the Heisman in 1961.

■

Emlen Tunnell was the first African-American coach in the NFL. Tunnell, a former defensive back for the N.Y. Giants, became a Giants' coach in 1965. Tunnell was also the first African-American player elected to the Pro Football Hall of Fame. He was inducted in 1967.

The first African-American to serve as head coach of a pro football team was Fritz Pollard. Pollard, a former All-Star halfback at Brown University, was co-head coach of the Akron Pros with Elgie Tobin in 1920.

■

Former National Football League linebacker Reggie Fowler became the first African-American owner of an NFL club in February of 2005, reaching an agreement to purchase the Minnesota Vikings. Fowler played linebacker for the University of Wyoming and briefly with the Cincinnati Bengals.

The New York Jets were the first team from the American Football League (now the AFC) to win a Super Bowl. The Jets, led by quarterback Joe Namath, beat the heavily-favored Baltimore Colts 16 to 7 in Super Bowl III, which was played in 1969.

■

Frank Filchock of the Washington Redskins was the first NFL quarterback to throw a 99-yard touchdown pass. On October 15, 1939, Filchock tossed a 99-yard T.D. reception to end Andy Farkas in a game against the Pittsburgh Steelers.

■

Quarterback John Elway was the first player picked in the 1983 National Football League Draft. He was selected by the Baltimore Colts and immediately traded to the Denver Broncos.

The Denver Broncos and the Boston Patriots (now the New England Patriots) met in the first regular season game played in the old American Football League (now part of the NFL). The Broncos played the Patriots on Friday night, September 9, 1960 at Boston University Field in Boston, Massachusetts. Denver won the game 13 to 10.

■

John Elway was the first member of the Denver Broncos to be voted into the Pro Football Hall of Fame. The Broncos' quarterback was inducted in August of 2004.

■

The first two quarterbacks named to the Pro Football Hall of Fame were Earl "Dutch" Clark of the Portsmouth Spartans and Detroit Lions and Sammy Baugh of the Washington Redskins. Clark and Baugh were inducted into the Pro Football Hall of Fame in 1963.

Sid Luckman of the Chicago Bears was the first NFL quarterback to pass for more than 400 yards in a single game. On November 14, 1943 Luckman passed for 433 yards in a 56 to 7 victory over the New York Giants.

■

Beattie Feathers of the Chicago Bears was the first NFL running back to gain 1,000 yards rushing in his rookie pro season. Feathers gained 1,004 yards in 1934, his first year as a player in the National Football League.

■

The National Football League's Rookie of the Year Award was first presented in 1955. The first winner of the award was running back Alan Ameche of the Baltimore Colts.

The Downtown Athletic Club of New York awarded the Heisman Trophy to college football's top player for the first time in 1935. The winner was running back Jay Berwanger of the University of Chicago.

■

The National Football League held its first amateur player draft in 1936. The first player selected as a number one draft choice was Jay Berwanger of the University of Chicago. Berwanger was selected by the Philadelphia Eagles.

■

John Jefferson of the San Diego Chargers was the first receiver in the history of the NFL to have three consecutive 1,000-yard receiving seasons in his first three years in the league. Jefferson established the mark in 1978, 1979, and 1980.

Tod Goodwin was the first New York Giant rookie player to lead the NFL in pass receiving. Rookie Goodwin made 26 catches in 1935 to lead the National Football League in receptions that year.

■

Bob Tucker of the New York Giants was the first tight end to ever lead the NFC in receiving. Tucker snared 59 passes in 1971 to lead the National Football League in receptions.

■

Tight end L.J. Smith of the Philadelphia Eagles caught his first NFL touchdown pass on December 7, 2003 in a game against the Dallas Cowboys. The pass was thrown by Eagles' Q.B. Donovan McNabb.

Wide receiver Harold Carmichael of the Philadelphia Eagles caught three touchdown passes in one game for the first time in his long career on November 9, 1980. Carmichael had three T.D. catches against the New Orleans Saints in a 34 to 21 victory for the Eagles.

■

The first player in NFL history to return a kickoff 106 yards for a touchdown was Al Carmichael of the Green Bay Packers. Carmichael returned a kick 106 yards for a score against the Chicago Bears on October 7, 1956.

■

Tom Dempsey was the first NFL place-kicker to boot a field goal more than 60 yards. On November 8, 1970 Tom Dempsey of the New Orleans Saints kicked a 63-yard field goal against the Los Angeles Rams.

Emmitt Smith of the Dallas Cowboys led the NFL in rushing for the first time in 1991. Smith rushed for 1,563 yards on 365 carries in 1991.

■

Defensive end Fred Dryer of the Los Angeles Rams was the first NFL player to record two safeties in a single game. On October 21, 1973, Dryer scored four points by twice tackling Green Bay Packer ballcarriers in their own end zone.

■

The first man to scoop up a fumble in a NFL game and run 98-yards with the ball for a touchdown was George Halas of the Chicago Bears. In a game against the Marion (Ohio) Oorang Indians on November 4, 1923, Halas picked up a fumble and returned it 98 yards for a score.

Vencie Glenn of the San Diego Chargers was the first NFL player to return an interception 103 yards for a score. Glenn intercepted a pass against the Denver Broncos in 1987 and raced 103 yards for a touchdown.

■

Jim Brown of the Cleveland Browns won his first of eight NFL rushing titles in 1957. Brown led the league in 1957 with 942 yards on 202 carries.

CHAPTER 2

ON THE GRIDIRON

Okay, team! It's time to check out the field of play. Stay in bounds as you examine football's rules, regulations, and terms as they evolve down through the years.

Now, just in case you're not already an expert on gridiron guidelines and pigskin history, we're also going to have a fun-filled skull session to explore the in's and out's of America's favorite fall sport. How was football invented? Why is a football field called a gridiron? Was a touchdown always worth six points? In addition, you'll learn how many present-day football strategies came about, explore highlights in football's rich history, and become acquainted with many famous figures.

Most of the early football games in America were played in and around the city of Boston, Massachusetts. Early in football's development, the sport was sometimes called "The Boston Game."

■

Football was so popular in Massachusetts, America's first formal football organization, "The Oneida Football Club," was formed in Boston in 1862.

■

The first rugby-style football contest played between college teams took place in 1874. Students from McGill University in Canada visited Boston to play football against students from Harvard University.

■

A round ball was first used for early football games. In 1875, an egg-shaped leather ball was put into use.

HOW FOOTBALL EVOLVED

American football evolved from the sports of soccer and rugby. The sport called soccer in the United States is still known as football throughout much of the world.

■

It wasn't until the 1880's that a great rugby player from Yale, Walter Camp, pioneered rules changes that slowly transformed rugby into the new game of American Football.

■

The game of rugby was accidentally invented in England during a game of soccer between students at Rugby School. In 1823, a student named William Webb Ellis broke the rules of soccer and picked up the ball while a game was in progress. Ellis started to run away with the ball. Other students tried to tackle him to get the ball back. Tackling a ballcarrier proved to be so much fun a new sport was born. This "Rugby Game" became the official sport call "Rugby."

In 1882, a football team on offense had three downs to advance the ball five yards in order to get a first down. This changed in 1912, when a rule change gave offensive football teams four downs to advance the ball ten yards in order to secure a first down.

■

A touchdown was only worth a single point in 1883. In 1884, it was increased from one point to four points. Then in 1912 it was officially given its current point value of six points.

■

In 1883, a "conversion" (PAT kick today) counted as four points instead of just one.

Field goals in football counted as five points in 1883. It was reduced from five points to four points in 1904. For the first time in football history, running the ball over the goal-line became more important than kicking a ball over the crossbar. (Note: A touchdown was still worth five points in 1904.)

■

Finally, in 1909, a field goal was finally reduced in value to its current point value of three points.

■

A new rule implemented in 1910 required seven offensive blockers to line up on the line of scrimmage at the start of play.

■

Football games were broken down into four quarters for the first time in 1910.

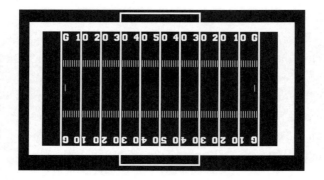

The American Intercollegiate Football Association was formed in 1876. It served as the governing body of schools who wanted to play football under rugby rules.

■

In 1877, football teams utilized a dangerous offensive maneuver known as "the Flying Wedge." A ballcarrier ran behind a group of players who locked arms to form a human V-shaped wall. The Flying Wedge rumbled forward, smashing down and trampling would-be tacklers. The Flying Wedge formation resulted in many serious injuries and even some deaths.

The Flying Wedge formation was outlawed in 1894.

■

Walter Camp, who excelled in football, track, tennis, swimming, rowing, and baseball at Yale University, is known as "the Father of Football" for his many contributions to the game.

■

Stripes were painted on football fields for the first time in 1882.

■

From a distance, early football fields looked like a large cooking utensil with thin, metal bars used to grill meat called a "gridiron." A football field was nicknamed a "gridiron" for that reason.

A star player for Princeton University in 1888 was an athlete named Edgar Allan Poe. Poe was a direct descendant and namesake of the famous American writer Edgar Allan Poe. Six Poe brothers (Edgar Allan, Arthur, S. Johnson, Neilson, Gresham, and John) eventually played football at Princeton in the early days of the sport.

■

The popularity of football spread from the northeast coast of America to the South, West, and Midwest during the 1890's.

■

The first college football game on America's West Coast was played between Stanford University and the University of California in 1892.

The Southern Intercollegiate Association was formed in 1894 to govern college sports, including football. Members of the Association were Georgia, Alabama, Georgia Tech, Vanderbilt, North Carolina, and Sewanee (later called the University of the South).

■

The Western (Football) Conference was formed in 1895. Its members included Illinois, Wisconsin, Purdue, Northwestern, Minnesota, Chicago and Lake Forest, which was soon replaced by Michigan. (Indiana, Ohio State, and Iowa were also added to the membership a short time later.)

■

In 1897, an 18-year-old footballer at the University of Georgia named Richard V. Gammon died on a football field from injuries he suffered during a game. His death started a public outcry to outlaw the game of football in America.

The University of Michigan started a winning streak on the gridiron in 1901 that lasted for 56 straight games.

■

In 1905, football once again became the target of protestors in America. A noted sportswriter named Bill Stern announced to the public that according to his calculations, 35 young athletes had died over the last 36 years as a direct result of football injuries.

■

In the early 20th century, American football were noted for serious injuries, as well as the deaths of a significant number of players. President Theodore Roosevelt threatened to outlaw football if the game could not be made safer. In 1905, representatives from sixty schools across America met to draw up a list of rules and regulations to make football a safer game. The focus of football games consequently shifted from brute force and violence to skilled, athletic execution.

West Virginia Wesleyan was one of the first schools to utilize the forward pass in football.

■

Northwestern University and the University of Notre Dame popularized the passing game in football during the 1908 season.

■

The American Intercollegiate Football Rules Committee became the National Collegiate Athletic Association (NCAA) in 1910. The NCAA still governs all college sports to this day.

■

Coach Glenn "Pop" Warner, the football coach at the Carlisle Indian School in Pennsylvania, invented the "single wing" formation in 1910. It revolutionized offensive football.

1. Sometimes a quarterback steps up to the line of scrimmage and calls an audible.

    What is an audible?

■

2. If a quarterback is a drop-back passer, he will try to stay in the pocket.

    What is the pocket?

■

3. No football enjoys getting sacked.

    What is a sack?

■

4. A smart quarterback is always on the lookout for a blitz?

    What is a blitz?

Answers

1. An "audible" is a quarterback's vocal signal at the line of scrimmage which changes the set play he originally called in the huddle to a different play.

2. The pocket in football is a small area formed behind blockers where the quarterback is protected from onrushing defenders while he attempts to locate a receiver to throw the ball to.

3. A "sack" in football is when a QB attempting to pass is tackled by a defender before he can throw the ball.

4. A "blitz" is an all-out defensive charge at a quarterback attempting to pass by linebackers and/or defensive backs.

ON THE FIELD

A modern American football field is 120 yards long and 53⅓ yards wide.

■

A football field measures 100 yards from goal-line to goal-line. Each end zone is ten yards deep.

■

White stripes are painted across a football field every five yards.

■

The middle stripe on a football field is the 50 yard line. From the 50 yard line, numbers are painted every ten yards (40, 30, 20, 10) to the goal lines.

■

Goal posts are located at opposite ends of the field and are centered in the middle of the football field. The crossbar section of a goalpost is ten feet above the ground.

A modern football is a leather-covered tan or brown ball.

■

A regulation football is oval-shaped and weighs between 14 and 15 ounces. It is inflated to a pressure of 12½ to 13½ pounds.

■

Some football leagues for youngsters use footballs that are smaller than regulation size footballs.

Football games are divided into two halves of 30 minutes each. Each half is made up of two 15-minute quarters. A football game is four quarters long.

■

There is a 15-minute (sometimes longer for special occasions) break between the two halves of a football game. This break is called "halftime."

■

Each half of a football game starts with a kickoff. Teams also kick off after each score.

■

A coin flip or toss determines who will kick off at the start of a game. The team that wins the coin toss can choose to kick the ball, receive the ball or defend a specific end of the field. The winner can also defer making its choice until the start of the second half.

There are seven officials in an NFL football game. They are the referee (who is in charge), an umpire, a linesman, a field judge, a back judge, a line judge, and a side judge.

■

A personal foul in football results in a 15-yard penalty against the guilty team.

■

Offsetting penalties means that both teams have committed fouls which cancel each other out.

■

A player is "off-sides" if he moves over the line of scrimmage before a play starts or if he lines up over the neutral zone established by the set position of the football prior to play. Being off-sides results in a five-yard penalty.

An "onside kick" is a special type of kickoff normally utilized when the kicking team is losing late in the game. The purpose of an onside kick is to recover possession of the ball so the kicking team can go back on offense. The ball is kicked a short distance of at least ten yards in the hope that a member of the kicking team will be able to recover it. (A kick that travels at least ten yards is a free ball.)

■

A "fair catch" is made when a player about to catch a punted ball waves his arm in the air to indicate he will not advance the ball in exchange for being given the opportunity to field the punt unmolested by defenders.

■

A "fumble" is when a ballcarrier loses control of a ball in his possession and drops it. A fumbled ball is a free ball.

WHAT'S HIS NUMBER?

Football players wear numbered jerseys. A player's number normally corresponds to the position he plays.

■

A football quarterback normally wears a single digit number or a number in the teens. Quarterback Joe Theismann of the Washington Redskins wore number seven (7).

■

Q.B. Eli Manning of the New York Giants wears number ten (10).

■

Fullbacks in football usually wear numbers in the thirties. Fullback Jim Brown of the Cleveland Browns wore number thirty-two (32).

■

Football numbers in the twenties or forties are normally given to defensive backs and running backs. Cornerback Ray Mickens of the New York Jets wears number twenty-four (24).

Halfback Larry Brown of the Washington Redskins wore number forty-three (43).

■

A center in football usually wears a number in the fifties or sixties. Center Chuck Bednarik of the Philadelphia Eagles wore number fifty-one (51). Buffalo Bills' center, Kent Hull, wore number sixty-seven (67).

Pro Hall-of-Fame center Jim Otto of the Oakland Raiders wore the number double zero (00).

■

In football, offensive guards usually wear numbers in the sixties. Guard Gene Upshaw of the Oakland Raiders wore number sixty-three (63).

■

Offensive and defensive tackles in football normally have numbers in the seventies. Defensive tackle Bob Lilly, of the Dallas Cowboys, wore number seventy-four (74).

Tight ends in football are usually given numbers in the eighties. Tight end Mike Ditka of the Chicago Bears and Dallas Cowboys wore number eighty-nine (89).

■

On defense, linebackers in football normally wear numbers in the fifties or nineties. Linebacker Lawrence Taylor of the N.Y. Giants wore number fifty-six (56). Linebacker Kevin Greene of the Carolina Panthers wore number ninety-one (91).

CANADIAN FOOTBALL TIDBITS

A football playing field in Canada is 110 yards long by 65 yards wide.

■

In Canada, a football team on offense has three downs to advance the ball ten yards in order to secure a first down.

There are 12 players on each side in a Canadian football contest. On offense, the 12th player is a running back or receiver. On defense, the 12th player is a linebacker or a defensive back.

■

The "Grey Cup Trophy" is awarded to the winner of the Canadian Football League Championship.

■

Only a limited number of American football players are allowed on each professional football team in Canada.

CHAPTER 3

THE OLD COLLEGE TRY

Rah! Rah! Rah! If you're a fan of the Fighting Irish of Notre Dame, you might implore your favorite college squad to "win one for the Gipper." If the Nittany Lions of Penn State are the team you roar for, you just might don the team colors of blue and white and trust in the gridiron wisdom of Joe Paterno.

Of course, if the University of Alabama floods your senses with football memories, you might cry out "roll the Crimson Tide" and pray for a little heavenly intervention from Alabama's legendary coach Paul "Bear" Bryant. The truth is, college football is drenched with tradition. So never say die, forge ahead, and give it the old college try . . . just for the fun of it!

The University of Southern California (USC) shared college football's national championship with Louisiana State University (LSU) in 2003.

■

Halfback Marcus Allen of the University of Southern California won the Heisman Trophy as America's top college football player in 1981. Allen rushed for 2,427 yards and 23 touchdowns that season.

■

Peyton Manning of the University of Tennessee won the Davey O'Brien Award as America's top college football quarterback in 1997. Manning threw 89 touchdown passes during his college career.

■

The team colors of the University of Tennessee are orange and white. The Tennessee team is nicknamed the "Volunteers."

JIM THORPE: ALL EVERYTHING

Jim Thorpe was one of the greatest college football players of all time. Thorpe was a Native American who played at the Carlisle Indian School in Pennsylvania in the early 1900's.

■

Jim Thorpe's college football coach at the Carlisle School for Indians was the legendary Glenn "Pop" Warner.

■

In 1911 and 1912, Jim Thorpe was named an All-American football player.

■

In addition to his football heroics, Jim Thorpe won gold medals in both the decathlon and pentathlon at the 1912 Olympic Games.

Jim Thorpe was part Sac and Fox, part Pottawatomie, and part Kickapoo. His tribal name was "Wa-Tho-Huck," which means "bright path."

■

Jim Thorpe was an outstanding running back and field goal kicker. In 1911, Thorpe single-handedly outscored a great Yale team which didn't lose another game until 1915. When Carlisle beat Yale 18 to 15 in 1911, Thorpe scored a touchdown and kicked field goals of 15, 22, 34, and 48 yards.

■

In a 1950 Associated Press poll, Jim Thorpe was voted the "Greatest Athlete of the First Half-Century."

The forward pass was legalized in college football in 1906.

■

The Army football team of 1914 won the National Championship.

■

Cornell's football team was declared the national champion by Walter Camp in 1915.

■

The University of Washington football team, coached by Gil Dobie, had its amazing 61-game winning streak ended in 1916.

■

Glenn "Pop" Warner played his college football at Cornell University, where he was a pre-law student.

Pop Warner coached college football for 44 years and won 319 games.

■

The nickname of the Miami (of Florida) football team is the Hurricanes. Its team colors are orange, green, and white.

■

Brigham Young University is known as the Cougars. Royal blue and white are the Cougar's team colors.

The West Virginia team is known as the Mountaineers. Its team colors are old gold and blue.

■

The University of Oklahoma football squad is nicknamed the Sooners. The Sooners' team colors are crimson and cream.

■

The University of Arkansas is known as the Razorbacks. Its team colors are cardinal and white.

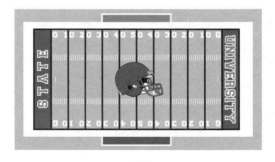

FOOTBALL NAME GAME

Try your best on this college football team nickname test. Match each school with its correct nickname:

1. Ohio State   A. Golden Bears
2. Wisconsin   B. Longhorns
3. Florida State   C. Wolverines
4. California   D. Seminoles
5. Michigan   E. Buckeyes
6. Texas   F. Badgers

Hooray! Here are the answers:
1. E (The Ohio State Buckeyes)
2. F (The Wisconsin Badgers)
3. D (The Florida State Seminoles)
4. A (The California Golden Bears)
5. C (The Michigan Wolverines)
6. B (The Texas Longhorns)

NOTRE DAME TIDBITS

Quarterback Gus Dorias and end Knute Rockne of the University of Notre Dame formed the most famous passing combination in college football during the early 1900's.

■

Notre Dame's revolutionary passing attack in 1913 won national acclaim after the Fighting Irish used key pass completions to beat a previously undefeated Army squad 35 to 13 that season.

■

Knute Rockne of Notre Dame was an All-American end in 1913.

■

Knute Rockne was the head coach of Notre Dame for 13 years. During that time he won 105 games and lost only 12 games.

From 1922 to 1924, Notre Dame had a famous backfield made up of halfbacks Don Miller and Jim Crowley, fullback Elmer Layden and quarterback Harry Stuhldreher. Together Miller, Crowley, Layden and Stuhldreher became known as "the Four Horsemen of Notre Dame," because of the way they executed tricky shifts on the field.

After Notre Dame's backfield led Coach Knute Rockne's "Fighting Irish" to a thrilling 13–7 win over a powerful Army football squad on October 18, 1924, Grantland Rice, the famous sportswriter, penned these immortal words:

"Outlined against a blue-gray October sky, the Four Horsemen rode again. In dramatic lore they are known as famine, pestilence, destruction and death. These are only aliases. Their real names are Stuhdreher, Miller, Crowley and Layden."

The most lopsided college football contest in history took place on October 7, 1916 at Grand Field in Atlanta, Georgia. Cumberland University of Tennessee lost to Georgia Tech by the score of 222 to 0.

■

The Georgia Tech team that defeated Cumberland University 222 to 0 in 1916 was coached by John Heisman, the man the Heisman Trophy is named after.

■

In 2004, there were 117 Division 1-A College football teams in America.

■

John Gagliardi, the football coach at St. John's College in Minnesota, coached for over 50 years in Division III and recorded over 400 football victories.

The Walter Payton Player of the Year Award has been given to the top Division 1-AA player in the country since 1987. The winner in 1987 was running back Kenny Gamble of Colgate University.

■

Coach Ron Harms of Texas A & M—Kingsville won 214 college football games at the Division II level.

Coach Larry Coker of the Miami Hurricanes won his first 24 games in a row as a head coach. His first career loss was to Ohio State in the 2003 Fiesta Bowl. Ohio State defeated Miami 31 to 21 in two periods of overtime.

■

Mount Union was the NCAA Division-AA Football Champion in 2003. Mount Union defeated Trinity 48 to 7 in the championship game.

Grambling University led all Division 1-AA football programs in scoring in 2003. Grambling scored 506 points in 13 games for an average of 38.92 points per football contest.

■

The Nebraska Cornhuskers once had a streak of 33 straight seasons where they won nine or more football games per season. The streak began in 1969 and ended in 2002.

■

Princeton University plays football in the Ivy League. The Ivy League is made up of teams from Princeton, Pennsylvania, Cornell, Dartmouth, Brown, and Columbia.

■

Tailback Dick Kazmaier is the first and only Princeton football player to ever win the Heisman Trophy. Kazmaier won the award in 1951.

"You play the way you practice."

Legendary football coach Glenn "Pop" Warner.

■

"Besides pride, loyalty, discipline, heart and mind, confidence is the key to all the locks."

Penn State football coach Joe Paterno.

■

"They say I teach brutal football, but the only thing brutal about football is losing."

Alabama football coach Paul "Bear" Bryant.

■

"It isn't necessary to say that a football team loses. I prefer the language of the Olympics in which you say somebody won second."

UCLA football coach Tommy Prothro.

"We will definitely be improved this year. Last year we lost ten games. This year we only scheduled nine."

Montana State football coach Ray Jenkins.

■

"Football is not a contact sport—it's a collision sport. Dancing is a contact sport."

Michigan State football coach Duffy Daugherty.

■

"Sometimes the light at the end of the tunnel is an oncoming train."

Arkansas, North Dame, and South Carolina football coach Lou Holtz.

■

"Never let life elude you. That is life's biggest fumble."

Illinois football coach Bob Zuppke.

Running back Ed Marinaro of Cornell led the nation in rushing in 1971 with 1,881 yards on 356 carries for an average of 209.00 yards per game. Marinaro finished second in the Heisman Trophy voting in 1971 to quarterback Pat Sullivan of Auburn, who was named the country's top player.

■

Outstanding halfback John Lattner of Notre Dame won the Heisman Trophy in 1953. Of all of the Heisman Award winners, he is one of the least well known to modern football fans.

■

Charles "Chic" Harley was Ohio State's first All-American player. He was named an All-American back in 1916 and is credited with helping turn Ohio State into a national football power.

■

John Hubbard was the first player from Amherst College to be named an All-American in football. He was an All-American back in 1905.

Paul Robeson was Rutgers' first All-American football player. He was also the first African-American player in football history to receive All-American honors in consecutive years. Robeson was an All-American end in 1917 and 1918.

■

It is believed that Princeton invented football cheerleading in 1870. In Princeton's second gridiron clash against state rival Rutgers, special "rooters" on the Princeton sidelines chanted, yelled, and shouted during the football game to distract the Rutgers players.

TWO LEGENDS OF THE GAME

Halfback Red Grange of the University of Illinois had a unique and elusive running style that earned him a famous nickname during the 1920's. Red Grange was known as "The Galloping Ghost." He was an All-American from 1923 to 1925, and wore the number seventy-seven (77) on his football jersey.

■

Red Grange's coach during his years at the University of Illinois was the legendary football mentor Bob Zuppke.

Football legend Bronislaw "Bronko" Nagurski played fullback on offense and tackle on defense for the University of Minnesota. He was an All-American at fullback and tackle in 1929.

■

Bronko Nagurski was one of college football's most feared runners and tacklers of all time. Famous sportswriter Grantland Rice once said this about Nagurski: "Bronko is the only man who ever lived who could lead his own interference."

■

Famous football coach Steven Owen once said this about Bronko: "There's only one defense that can stop Nagurski, shoot him before he leaves the dressing room."

After Rutgers defeated Princeton in college football's first game (in 1869), Princeton beat Rutgers every time the two teams met on the gridiron for the next 69 years.

■

In 1924, Red Grange scored four touchdowns in 12 minutes against a previously unbeaten Michigan football team. The Galloping Ghost scored on runs of 95 yards, 67 yards, 56 yards, and 44 yards the first four times he carried the pigskin. He later scored a fifth T.D. and passed for a sixth score in the University of Illinois victory.

■

Running back Ernie Nevers played football at Stanford for coach Pop Warner and was an All-American in 1923 and 1925. Nevers was injured in 1924 and missed most of the season.

Nebraska football coach Tom Osborne won 255 games and lost 49 during his 25-year coaching career.

■

Paul "Bear" Bryant is best remembered for being the head football coach at Alabama. Bryant also coached football at Maryland (1945), Kentucky (1946-53), and Texas A & M (1954-1957). Bear Bryant was the Alabama coach from 1958 to 1982.

The Butkus Award is presented annually by the Downtown Athletic Club of Orlando, Florida to the outstanding college football linebacker in America.

■

Linebacker Brian Bosworth of Oklahoma won the Butkus Award for his outstanding defensive play in 1985 and in 1986.

■

Dan Morgan was the first player from the University of Miami to win the Butkus Award. Morgan was named College Football's top linebacker in 2000.

■

The Hill Trophy honors the nation's Outstanding Division II College Football player. It was first presented in 1986 when the winner was quarterback Jeff Bentrim of North Dakota State.

The Outland Trophy is awarded to the most outstanding interior lineman in college football. It was first presented in 1946 when the winner was tackle George Connor of Notre Dame.

■

Quarterback Roger Staubach of Navy was the winner of the Heisman Trophy as college football's top player in 1963.

■

In 1945, fullback Felix "Doc" Blanchard of Army was named college football's best player and was awarded the Heisman Trophy.

■

In 1946, halfback Glenn Davis of Army was voted America's top college football player and won the Heisman Trophy.

College running backs Doc Blanchard and Glenn Davis of Army were known as "Mr. Inside and Mr. Outside" during the mid-1940's.

■

The Maxwell Award has been given annually to the top player in college football since 1937. Its first winner was halfback Clint Frank of Yale.

■

Running back Larry Johnson of Penn State won college football's Maxwell Award in 2002.

■

Halfback Johnny Lattner of Notre Dame is the only college football player to win the Maxwell Trophy two years in a row. Lattner won the award as college football's top player in 1952 and 1953.

The Thorpe Trophy is presented by the Jim Thorpe Athletic Club of Oklahoma City to college football's most outstanding defensive back. Its first winner was Thomas Everett of Baylor in 1986.

■

In 1988, cornerback Deion Sanders of Florida State won the Thorpe Award as the top defensive back in college football.

Defensive star Al Brosky of the University of Illinois intercepted 29 passes from 1950 to 1952 to set a college football record for career interceptions.

■

Oklahoma State running back Barry Sanders set a single season record by rushing for 2,628 yards in 11 games during the 1988 season.

Quarterback David Klinger of Houston established a single season mark by throwing 54 touchdown passes during the 1990 college football season.

■

Wisconsin running back Ron Dayne rushed for a record 6,397 yards in his college career, which began in 1996 and ended in 1999.

FORDHAM UNIVERSITY TIDBITS

Jim Crowley, the famous former Notre Dame halfback, was the head football coach at Fordham University (in New York) in 1937.

■

Fordham University's offensive line was so good in 1937 sportswriters dubbed them "The Seven Blocks of Granite" because no defense could push them aside.

■

Center Alex Wojciechowicz was the star member of the Seven Blocks of Granite. Wojciechowicz was an All-American offensive lineman in 1936 and 1937.

■

Legendary pro football coach Vince Lombardi played his college football at Fordham.

Football's T-formation first appeared on the gridiron in the 1930's. The T-formation is so-named because the backs are positioned in a way that resembles a letter "T" when viewed from a distance.

■

Coach Clark Shaughnessy and his Stanford football squad helped popularize football's T-formation. Stanford went undefeated and beat Nebraska 21 to 13 in the 1941 Rose Bowl using the T-formation.

Don Faurot of the University of Missouri was the coach who designed football's split-T formation. The new formation allowed college quarterbacks to run option plays.

■

The nickname of the University of Delaware is the "Fightin' Blue Hens."

Texas Christian University is known as the "Horned Frogs."

■

Coach Lou Little's Columbia Lions astounded the college football world in 1934 when Columbia defeated Stanford 7 to 0 in the 1934 Rose Bowl.

■

The Southern California Trojans, coached by Howard Jones, went undefeated in 32 games from 1931 to 1933.

■

End Don Hutson was an All-American at Alabama in 1934. Hutson is regarded as one of the greatest pass catchers in the history of college and pro football.

A PASSING GAME

To pass this college quarterback quiz match the following college QB's with the school each one played college football for.

1. Dan Marino
2. Doug Flutie
3. Michael Vick
4. Sonny Sixkiller
5. Drew Brees
6. Archie Manning

A. Boston College
B. University of Washington
C. Purdue
D. Virginia Tech
E. University of Mississippi
F. University of Pittsburgh

The correct completions are:

1. F (Dan Marino went to the University of Pittsburgh)
2. A (Doug Flutie went to Boston College)
3. D (Michael Vick went to Virginia Tech)
4. B (Sonny Sixkiller went to the University of Washington)
5. C (Drew Brees went to Purdue)
6. E (Archie Manning went to the University of Mississippi)

Clarence "Ace" Parker, who was an All-American halfback at Duke in 1936, is considered to be one of the best football players in Blue Devils history.

■

Tailback Frank Sinkwich of Georgia won the Heisman Trophy as college football's top player in 1942.

■

The University of Alabama has played in more than fifty college football bowl games.

Speedy running back Byron White of the University of Colorado is better known to football fans by his famous nickname. Bryon "Whizzer" White was an All-American in 1938.

■

Marshall University's nickname is the "Thundering Herd."

■

The University of Minnesota, coached by Bernie Bierman, won back-to-back national championships in football in 1940 and 1941.

■

Two-platoon football became popular in college football in 1941 when unlimited substitution of players became legal. Unlimited substitution meant teams could have one squad play defense and another play offense.

The University of Oregon football team is known as the "Ducks," while the Oregon State gridiron squad is nicknamed the "Beavers."

■

The College Football Hall of Fame was established in 1955 by the National Football Foundation. It is located in South Bend, Indiana.

■

Coaches Earl "Red" Blaik, Walter Camp, Gus Dorais, John Heisman, Knute Rockne, Amos Alonzo Stagg, Glenn "Pop" Warner, and Bob Zuppke are all members of the College Football Hall of Fame.

John L. Smith, the head football coach at Michigan State University in 2004, is an advocate of the running game. In 2001, Coach Smith ran with the bulls in Pamplona, Spain.

■

In 1986, halfback Paul Palmer of Temple University collected 2,633 yards in all-purpose running.

■

Receiver Howard Twilley of Tulsa made 95 catches in the 1964 college football season and caught 134 passes in the 1965 season.

■

Tyrone Willingham, the head football coach at the University of Notre Dame, was the first African-American head coach in any sport at Notre Dame.

The Army football team coached by Henry "Red" Blaik was undefeated in 1944, 1945, and 1946. Army was named the national champions of college football in 1944 and 1945.

■

In over 130 years of college football, neither Navy nor the Air Force Academy has even won a college football national championship.

■

Charles "Bud" Wilkinson, a former player at the University of Minnesota, became the head coach of the University of Oklahoma in 1947.

■

Bud Wilkinson won his first national championship as the head coach of Oklahoma in 1950. He also won national titles in 1955 and 1956.

College football's national championship was shared by two teams in 1970. Nebraska, coached by Bob Devaney, was declared the top team by the Associated Press, while Texas, coached by Darrell Royal, was named the national champion by United Press International.

■

In 1896, the University of Wisconsin won the first Big Ten Conference Championship.

■

Ben Schwartzwalder won fame as the head football coach at Syracuse University during the 1950's. In 1959, Schwartzwalder's undefeated Syracuse squad was named the national champion of college football.

EDDIE ROBINSON TIDBITS

Eddie Robinson was the head coach at Grambling for over 50 years.

■

More than 200 college football players coached by Eddie Robinson at Grambling went on to play pro football.

■

Eddie Robinson holds the football coaching record—professional as well as collegiate—for most games won, with 408.

■

Eddie Robinson is a member of the College Football Hall of Fame.

Jim Brown, one of the greatest running backs in football history, played for Ben Schwartzwalder at Syracuse University. Brown was an All-American in football and lacrosse at Syracuse.

■

In 1958, LSU (Louisiana State University) and the University of Iowa shared college football's national championship. LSU was 11 and 0 in 1958, and Iowa posted a season record of 8 wins, 1 loss, and 1 tie that same year.

■

In 1957, Auburn University, coached by Shug Jordan and led by end Jimmy Phillips, was declared the national champion of college football by the Associated Press. Auburn posted a record of 11 wins and no losses.

Ohio State, coached by Woody Hayes and led by fullback Bob White, was declared the national champion in 1957 by International United Press and the Football Writers Association. Ohio State was 9-1 and won the Rose Bowl (played January 1, 1958), beating the University of Oregon by the score of 10 to 7.

■

Lafayette College and Lehigh University (both in Pennsylvania) have met on the gridiron over 138 times. No two college football teams have played more games against each other.

■

The Atlantic Coast Conference has been playing football games since 1953. Duke and Maryland shared the first conference title.

Bobby Bowden coached Florida State to a perfect record of 12 wins and 0 losses in 1999.

■

John Polanski of Wake Forest led the nation in rushing in 1939 by gaining 882 yards on 137 carries.

■

The University of Michigan has won over 820 college football games.

CHAPTER 4

LET'S GO PRO!

Die-hard gridiron fans, some in bizarre outfits, some with painted faces, and others in ordinary attire cram into towering football stadiums on Sunday afternoons and Monday nights in the fall. Inside those massive sports arenas, they cheer star players who are paid large sums of money to perform athletic miracles. When you mix sportsshowmanship and razzle-dazzle athletic entertainment with hard-hitting pigskin play, you get modern professional football. It's not only a fan favorite, but also a sports business empire.

However, pro football wasn't always popular with the public. Star players were underpaid and teams folded due to lack of fan support. To truly go pro you have to explore the early days of the NFL and meet the games, first teams, and stars. So, let's go pro!

Professional football games were scheduled to be played on Sundays so the games would not compete for fans with college football games, which were normally played on Saturdays.

■

Most gridiron experts agree that William "Pudge" Heffelfinger, the ex-Yale All-American, was football's first paid player. However, some football historians claim Lawson Fiscus, a former Princeton star, was football's first professional athlete.

■

Early pro football teams were company-sponsored squads in small Midwestern towns. The teams were supported by the companies for publicity or promotional purposes. They used employees as players. The employees were given company-paid time to practice and play football.

One of the best company-sponsored pro football teams was the Decatur (Il.) Staleys. The Staleys eventually became the Chicago Bears and were original members of the NFL.

■

The first professional football game was played in Westmoreland County in Pennsylvania on August 31, 1895. The two teams involved were YMCA football teams from Latrobe, Pennsylvania and Jeannette, Pennsylvania. The winning team would claim a cash prize. Latrobe beat Jeannette 12 to 0 to collect the money. A football legend claims John Brailler, a former college footballer who later became a dentist in Pennsylvania, was paid ten dollars to play quarterback for the Latrobe gridiron club.

Lawson Fiscus was paid 20 dollars a game to play football for a team in Greensburg, Pennsylvania in 1893.

■

Another successful company-sponsored pro football team was the Acme Packers. They later became the Green Bay Packers and joined the NFL in 1921.

■

Bill Parcells was the head football coach of the Dallas Cowboys for the 2004 season.

■

Bill Belichick was the head coach of the New England Patriots in 2004.

■

Chuck Noll coached the Pittsburgh Steelers to four Super Bowl victories. The Steelers under Coach Noll won Super Bowl titles in 1975, 1976, 1979, and 1980.

CONFERENCE CALL

The National Football League is currently divided into two conferences. The conferences are the American Football Conference (AFC) and the National Football Conference (NFC).

■

Each conference in the current NFL is separated into four divisions. They are the East Division, the West Division, the North Division and the South Division.

■

In 2004, there were 32 teams in the National Football League.

■

The New York Jets, the New England Patriots, the Miami Dolphins, and the Buffalo Bills made up the East Division of the AFC in 2004.

The Oakland Raiders, the Denver Broncos, the San Diego Chargers, and the Kansas City Chiefs were the 2004 member teams of the AFC's West Division.

■

In 2004, the Pittsburgh Steelers, the Cleveland Browns, the Baltimore Ravens, and the Cincinnati Bengals made up the North Division of the American Football Conference.

■

The South Division of the American Football Conference was made up of the Tennessee Titans, the Indianapolis Colts, the Jacksonville Jaguars, and the Houston Texans in 2004.

■

The Philadelphia Eagles, the New York Giants, the Washington Redskins, and the Dallas Cowboys were the teams in the NFC's East Division for the 2004 season.

Weeb Ewbank was the first New York Jets coach to take his gridiron squad to the Super Bowl. The Jets, guided by Weeb Ewbank, defeated the Baltimore Colts, coached by Don Shula, 16 to 7 in Super Bowl III.

■

Of the 14 teams that comprised the American Professional Football Association in 1920, only two original teams are currently still in the NFL. They are the Arizona Cardinals (formerly the Chicago Cardinals) and the Chicago Bears (formerly the Decatur Staleys).

■

The Columbus (Ohio) Panhandlers, the Providence (Rhode Island) Steamrollers, and the Pottsville (Pennsylvania) Maroons were early members of the National Football League.

The first night game in pro football history was played in Elmira, New York on November 21, 1902. The Philadelphia Athletics Football team defeated the Kanaweola Athletic Club gridiron squad by the score of 39 to 0.

■

The 1902 Philadelphia Athletics Pro Football team was owned by Connie Mack, who also owned pro baseball's Philadelphia Athletics.

■

Fullback Willie Heston of the University of Michigan is considered pro football's first holdout. In 1905, Heston wanted early pro teams to bid against each other for his services. When the teams declined to do so, Willie Heston refused to play pro football.

■

In 1906, Willie Heston played two games for the Canton Bulldogs and was paid six hundred dollars. Heston's pro football career abruptly ended when he broke his leg.

Football players did not sign binding contracts to play for pro teams in the early days. Some players jumped from team to team when they were offered higher pay. It was rumored that Knute Rockne once played for six different pro football teams in a single season.

■

In 1906, Eddie Wood of the Canton Bulldogs caught the first pass ever completed in a pro football game.

■

Former All-American Jim Thorpe was a star player for pro football's Canton Bulldogs in the early 1920's.

■

Former Notre Dame teammates Gus Dorais and Knute Rockne played quarterback and end (respectively) for the Massillon Tigers in the early days of pro football.

■

The American Professional Football Association was formed in 1920. The price of a team membership in the new pro league was one hundred dollars.

Jim Thorpe was elected the first president of the American Professional Football Association. He was president of the league and played in it.

■

The first pro football player deal took place in 1920. The Buffalo Bisons paid the Akron Pros three hundred dollars to acquire player Bob Nash.

■

Jim Thorpe organized a pro football team made up entirely of Native American gridiron stars. The team was known as the Oorang Indians and played professional football in 1921 and 1922.

■

Curly Lambeau, who had played with George Gipp at the University of Notre Dame, was one of the founding fathers of the Green Bay Packers.

BEAR FACTS

In 1921, pro football's Decatur Staleys team was taken over by player/coach George Halas. Halas moved the team to Chicago and renamed the club the Chicago Bears.

The Chicago Bears were the first pro team to practice every day.

Harold "Red" Grange, the famous "Galloping Ghost," became a member of the Chicago Bears in 1925.

Red Grange was the highest paid player in the NFL in 1925. Grange earned an estimated $125,000 in his first year as a pro football star.

Bronko Nagurski played for the Chicago Bears from 1930 to 1938. Nagurski was an All-Pro fullback in 1932, 1933, and 1934.

Bronko Nagurski threw a touchdown pass to Red Grange in a 1932 playoff game against the Portsmouth (Ohio) Spartans to give the Chicago Bears the NFL Championship.

In 1943, Bronko Nagurski came out of retirement to play one final season for the Chicago Bears. He helped the Bears win the NFL Championship that season.

George Halas coached the Chicago Bears for 40 seasons. He won 324 games, lost 151 games, and tied 31 gridiron contests.

Later in life, George Halas of the Chicago Bears was known by his famous football nickname, which was "Papa Bear" Halas.

TRUE OR FALSE?

The true test of a pro football fan is knowing which claims to fame are false and which are not. Try your hand at the following statements.

1. True or false? Quarterback Bret Favre of the Green Bay Packers has never thrown a 99-yard touchdown pass.

2. True or false? The Pittsburgh Steelers and the Philadelphia Eagles once merged into a single pro team known as the Phil-Pitt Steagles.

3. True or false? Quarterback John Elway of the Denver Broncos threw more touchdown passes during his NFL career then Q.B. Joe Montana of the San Francisco 49ers did.

4. True or false? Running back Herschel Walker rushed for over 10,000 yards during his NFL career.

Answers

1. False! QB Bret Favre of the Packers tossed a 99-yard T.D. toss to Robert Brooks in a game against the Chicago Bears in 1995.

2. True. In 1943, when the Pittsburgh Steelers and the Philadelphia Eagles were in financial difficulty, they merged into one team to survive. The Phil-Pitt Steagles were in existence for a single season.

3. True. John Elway of the Broncos tossed 300 touchdown passes in his 17-year NFL career. Joe Montana of the 49ers threw 273 touchdown passes during his 15 years in the NFL.

4. False. Herschel Walker, who played for the Dallas Cowboys, Minnesota Vikings and Philadelphia Eagles during his 12-year NFL career, rushed for a total of 8,225 yards.

The Green Bay Packers began as a pro football team located in Green Bay, Wisconsin and have never moved from their original home site.

■

The New York Giants became part of the National Football League in 1925.

■

In 1926, a rival pro football league known as the American Football League came into existence for a single season.

■

There were only eight teams in the National Football League in 1932. Those teams were the Boston Braves, the Brooklyn Dodgers, the Chicago Bears, the Chicago Cardinals, the New York Giants, the Green Bay Packers, the Portsmouth Spartans, and the Staten Island Stapletons.

In the 1930's, George Preston Marshall, a part owner of the Boston Braves NFL franchise, came up with the idea of amusing pro football fans at halftime by staging halftime shows.

■

Fan attendance for pro football games was so low in 1926 that 10 of the NFL's 22 teams went bankrupt. NFL teams had a roster of only 18 players in 1929.

■

The first NFL championship game between divisional winners was played on December 17, 1933 in Chicago. The Chicago Bears beat the New York Giants 23 to 21.

■

For winning the 1933 NFL Championship, each member of the victorious Chicago Bears team received a bonus check for $210.34.

■

On his first play as a professional football player, receiver Don Hutson of the Green Bay Packers caught an 83-yard touchdown pass. It happened in 1935 in a game against the N.Y. Giants.

Jay Berwanger, the winner of the Heisman Trophy in 1935, was the first player selected in the very first NFL draft, which was held in 1936. Berwanger was picked by the Philadelphia Eagles, but decided not to play professional football.

■

In 1937, quarterback Sammy Baugh of Texas Christian University signed a pro contract with the Washington Redskins and led the NFL in passing his rookie year. Baugh passed for 1,127 yards and 8 touchdowns in 1937.

■

In 1938, Byron "Whizzer" White of Colorado joined the Pittsburgh Steelers and led the NFL in rushing his first year as a pro player. White rushed for 567 yards in 1938 and scored four touchdowns.

■

A team franchise in the NFL had risen to the price of $50,000 in 1940.

One of the most lopsided NFL championship games in history took place in 1940. The Chicago Bears, led by QB Sid Luckman, crushed the Washington Redskins 73 to 0 to win the NFL title. The Washington Redskins gained a total of just three yards in the championship contest.

■

In 1941, Elmer Layden, who had won college football fame as one of the Four Horsemen of Notre Dame, served as Commissioner of the National Football League.

■

A second edition of the American Football League played games in 1936 and 1937. After a three-year gap, a third edition of the American Football League returned for the 1940 and 1941 seasons. After 1941, the AFL once again suspended operations.

■

During World War II, 638 pro football players served in the Armed Forces.

Sixty-nine NFL players were decorated for their service during WWII. Twenty-one NFL players lost their lives fighting for freedom in WWII.

■

The All-America Football Conference, a rival league of the NFL, was in existence from 1946 to 1949. It folded in after 1949 due to lack of fan support and three teams from the All-America Football Conference became members of the National Football League. The three teams were the Cleveland Browns, the Baltimore Colts, and the San Francisco 49ers.

■

The Cleveland Browns, coached by Paul Brown, won every All-America Football Conference Championship from 1946 to 1949.

■

Quarterback George Blanda began his pro football career in 1949 as a member of the Chicago Bears. Blanda went on to play 26 seasons of pro football as a signal-caller and place-kicker.

The Cleveland Browns won the NFL championship their first year in the league. In 1950, Cleveland defeated the Los Angeles Rams 30 to 28 to claim the NFL title. The NFL's first Pro Bowl as played in 1951. The All-Star grid contest was the idea of George P. Marshall, a part owner of the Washington Redskins.

■

Otto Graham, the quarterback of the Cleveland Browns, was the Most Valuable Player in the 1951 NFL Pro Bowl.

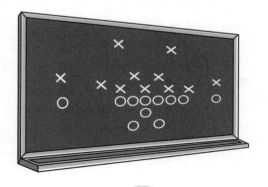

NFL linebacker Chuck Bednarik of the Philadelphia Eagles earned MVP honors in the 1954 Pro Bowl.

■

Running back Ollie Matson of the St. Louis Cardinals was named the most valuable player of the 1956 NFL Pro Bowl.

■

The NFL Players Association was formed in 1956.

■

Frank "Gunner" Gatski played offensive center for the Cleveland Browns in 1954 when the Browns beat the Detroit Lions 56 to 10 to win the NFL championship. Garski was later cut by Cleveland.

■

In 1957, Gunner Gatski played center for the Detroit Lions when they beat the Cleveland Browns 59 to 14 to win the NFL title that year.

■

In 1961, Canton, Ohio was chosen as the site of the Pro Football Hall of Fame.

The new American Football League was formed in 1959. The league was the brainchild of Lamar Hunt, a former end for Southern Methodist University and the son of billionaire H.L. Hunt.

■

The first NFL expansion team to win the first league game it ever played was the Minnesota Vikings, who did it on their season opener in 1961.

■

The New York Titans football team changed its name to the New York Jets in 1963.

■

Quarterback Joe Namath of the New York Jets was nicknamed "Broadway Joe" because of his flamboyant style on and off the gridiron.

■

In 1971, end Alan Page of the Minnesota Vikings became the first defensive player to win the NFL's Most Valuable Player award.

After his retirement, quarterback Eddie LeBaron of the Washington Redskins was asked to reflect on his NFL career.

LeBaron replied, "I had fun during my eleven NFL seasons. It was a fantastic experience, one I wouldn't have traded for anything."

■

Tampa Bay Buccaneers' coach John McKay once was asked how he evaluated a player's performance.

McKay replied, "I'm a big believer in the mirror test. All that matters is if you can look in the mirror and honestly tell the person you see there, that you've done your best."

Defensive end Jim Marshall of the Minnesota Vikings once was asked what's it like to be a pro football player.

Marshall replied, "A man who is a professional has had to play with a great deal of pain at one time or another. Such a man has a lot of pride about what he can do within himself, of the great sacrifice he can make. It helps him feel that he can tolerate that which the ordinary man can't tolerate, mentally and physically."

■

Years ago, San Diego Chargers' quarterback Dan Fouts was asked if anything new was being added to his team's famous passing attack.

Fouts replied, "Yeah. We're working on the spiral."

■

New Orleans running back George Rogers once was asked if he had any personal goals for the upcoming NFL season.

Rogers replied, "I want to gain 1,500 or 2,000 yards, whichever comes first."

In 1961, Canton, Ohio was chosen as the site of the Pro Football Hall of Fame.

■

In 1925, Norm Barry coached the Chicago Cardinals to the NFL Championship.

■

Buddy Parker coached the Detroit Lions to NFL championships in 1952 and 1953.

After the World Football League was formed, it lasted only a little more than one year as a professional sports league. In 1974, the Birmingham Americans won the WFL title by beating the Florida Blazers 22 to 21 in the championship game.

■

The Tampa Bay Buccaneers first played in the NFL during the 1976 season.

■

John Madden was the head football coach of the Oakland Raiders from 1969 to 1978.

■

From 1976 to 1980, cornerback Dave Brown was the only member of the Seattle Seahawks team to start every one of his team's NFL games.

■

Harold Carmichael of the Philadelphia Eagles caught at least one pass in 127 consecutive NFL games. His streak came to an end during the 1980 NFL season.

Quarterback Warren Moon of the Edmonton Eskimos was named the Most Outstanding Player in the Canadian Football League for the 1983 season.

■

The United States Football League began playing games in 1983. The league suspended operations after the 1985 season.

■

The Most Valuable Player of the NFL Pro Bowl in 1985 was defensive end Mark Gastineau of the New York Giants.

■

Running back Bo Jackson of Auburn was the number one draft pick of the NFL in 1986. Jackson was selected by the Tampa Bay Buccaneers.

■

In 1987, a 24-day pro football players' strike shortened the NFL season by one game. Replacement players were used by teams in place of veteran players.

The Arena Football League played its first pro contests in 1987.

■

The San Francisco 49ers, coached by Bill Walsh, defeated the Chicago Bears, coached by Mike Ditka, in the 1988 NFC Championship. The score of the game was 49ers 28 and Bears 3.

Running back Jerome Bettis of the St. Louis Rams was named the NFL's Offensive Rookie of the Year in 1993 by the Associated Press.

■

The San Francisco 49ers led the National Football Conference in total offense in 1998 with 6,800 yards.

The Denver Broncos led the American Football Conference in total offense in 1998 with 6,092 yards.

■

The XFL was created in 2001. It existed as a professional football league for only one year. In 2001, the Los Angeles Xtreme beat the San Francisco Demons 38 to 6 to claim the XFL's only championship.

■

Kansas City Chiefs' running back Priest Holmes was named the NFL's Offensive Player of the Year by the Associated Press in 2002.

Marvin Harrison of the Indianapolis Colts caught 143 passes for 1,722 yards and 11 touchdowns during the 2002 NFL season.

■

The Montreal Alouettes won the Canadian Football League's Grey Cup Championship in 2002. Montreal defeated the Edmonton Eskimos 25 to 16 in the title game.

■

Milt Stegall of the Winnipeg Blue Bombers was named the Canadian Football League's Most Valuable Player for the 2002 season.

■

Quarterback Mark Brunell of the Jacksonville Jaguars passed for 2,788 yards and 17 touchdowns during the 2002 NFL season.

■

In 2002, the Houston Texans became the second expansion team in NFL history to win its very first league game. The Texans beat the Dallas Cowboys 19 to 10 on opening day.

Quarterback Rich Gannon of the Oakland Raiders had ten 300-yard passing games during the 2002 NFL season.

■

Eric Moulds led the Buffalo Bills in receiving in 2002 by catching 100 passes for 1,287 yards and ten touchdowns.

Kicker Matt Stover led the Baltimore Ravens in scoring in 2002 with a total of 96 points.

■

Adam Vinatieri of the New England Patriots kicked the longest field goal of the 2002 NFL season. On November 10, 2002 Vinatieri booted a 57-yarder against the Chicago Bears.

■

Defensive end Julius Peppers of the Carolina Panthers was named the NFL's Defensive Player of the Year by the Associated Press in 2002.

In 2002, linebacker Derrick Brooks of the Tampa Bay Buccaneers was voted the Defensive Player of the Year in the NFL by the Associated Press.

■

Ricky Williams of the Miami Dolphins led the NFL in rushing in 2002. Williams gained 1,853 yards on 383 carries for an average of 4.8 yards per carry.

Steve McNair passed for 3,387 yards and 22 touchdowns playing quarterback for the Tennessee Titans during the 2002 NFL season.

■

Deuce McAllister scored the most touchdowns for the New Orleans Saints football squad in 2002. McAllister totaled 18 touchdowns for the Saints.

■

Quarterback Michael Vick of the Atlanta Falcons rushed for 777 yards in 2002.

■

Pittsburgh Steelers quarterback Tommy Maddox passed for 473 yards and 4 touchdowns against the Atlanta Falcons on November 10, 2002.

■

Quarterback Carson Palmer of U.S.C. was the top NFL draft pick in 2003. Palmer was selected by the Cincinnati Bengals.

The World Bowl Game, which is the championship of the NFL Europe, was won by the Frankfurt Galaxy in 2003. Doug Graber was the head coach of the winning team. Running back Jonas Lewis of the Frankfurt Galaxy was named the MVP of the game.

■

Barry Sanders, the star running back of the Detroit Lions, was voted into the Pro Football Hall of Fame in 2004.

■

In 2004, Ricky Williams, the Miami Dolphins' top running back, suddenly decided to retire from pro football.

■

Forty-year old veteran signal caller Vinny Testaverde was the starting quarterback for the Dallas Cowboys on opening day of the 2004 NFL season.

During the 2004 season, wide receiver Jerry Rice became the first player in the history of the National Football League to have 200 career T.D. catches.

■

The year 2004 was Minnesota Vikings' place-kicker Morten Andersen's 23rd year in the NFL.

■

Legendary coach Joe Gibbs returned to the NFL in 2004 as the head coach of the Washington Redskins.

■

Wide receiver Ricky Proehl of the Carolina Panthers, defensive safety Shawn Mayer of the New England Patriots, and offensive center Shaun O'Hara of the New York Giants all played high school football at Hillsborough High School in New Jersey.

The starting quarterback for the New York Giants on opening day of the 2004 NFL season was veteran Kurt Warner. Warner's backup was rookie Eli Manning.

■

A rule change in the National Football League in 2004 allowed head coaches to directly call timeouts.

CHAPTER 5

SUPER FEATS

It's the pinnacle of pro pigskin play, the zenith of gridiron greatness, professional football's finest contest. It's the Super Bowl!

The history of the Super Bowl starts way back in 1967 as a grudge match between the champions of two rival leagues. Pro football's super contest was created to crown a world champion and to settle a furious football fan debate. Which league was better? Was it the upstart American Football League or the much older National Football League?

The answers to that question and many others are revealed in the following pages. Fantastic facts about all your favorite Super Bowl players, coaches and teams await. So, get ready for some super football fun and read on.

Lamar Hunt, the owner of the Kansas City Chiefs, is the man who named the championship game between the American Football League and the National Football League the "Super Bowl."

■

A total of 61,946 fans attended Super Bowl I to watch the Green Bay Packers beat the Kansas City Chiefs 35 to 10. That game was not a sell-out.

■

Len Dawson was the starting quarterback for the Kansas City Chiefs in Super Bowl I.

■

Famous football tough guy Ray Nitschke was a star middle linebacker for the Green Bay Packers in Super Bowl I.

■

Bart Starr, who was named the MVP of Super Bowl I, was the 199th player selected in the 1956 NFL Draft.

Max McGee, who caught the first touchdown pass in Super Bowl history, was in the championship game only because regular Green Bay receiver Boyd Dowler was injured.

■

Curtis McClinton of the Kansas City Chiefs was the first AFL player to score a touchdown in a Super Bowl. McClinton caught a 7-yard toss from QB Len Dawson in the second period of Super Bowl I.

■

Kansas City Chiefs place-kicker Mike Mercer booted the first field goal in Super Bowl history. Mercer kicked a 31-yarder in the second period of Super Bowl I.

■

Max McGree of the Green Bay Packers caught only four passes for 91 yards during the 1966 regular season. In the 1967 Super Bowl (I), he snared seven passes for 138 yards and two touchdowns.

The Green Bay Packers collected $15,000 per man for winning Super Bowl I. The Kansas City Chiefs collected $7,500 per man for losing the world championship.

■

Super Bowl II was played in the Orange Bowl in Miami, Florida on January 14, 1968.

■

The AFL Champion Oakland Raiders met the NFL Champion Green Bay Packers in Super Bowl II.

■

The head coach of the Oakland Raiders when they played in Super Bowl II was John Rauch.

■

Receiver Boyd Dowler caught a 62-yard touchdown pass from Green Bay quarterback Bart Starr in Super Bowl II.

Don Chandler kicked four field goals for the Green Bay Packers in Super Bowl II. He was good on kicks of 39 yards, 20 yards, 43 yards, and 31 yards.

■

Kicker Don Chandler of the Green Bay Packers played in two Super Bowls and booted four field goals and eight extra points to tally a total of 20 points in Super Bowl play.

■

Center Jim Otto and guard Gene Upshaw were offensive linemen for the Oakland Raiders in Super Bowl II.

■

Defensive back Herb Adderley of the Green Bay Packers was the first player to return an interception for a touchdown in a Super Bowl. Adderley scored on a 60-yard interception return in Super Bowl II.

Daryle Lamonica was the starting QB for the Oakland Raiders in Super Bowl II. His backup was veteran George Blanda.

■

Signal-caller Bart Starr of the Green Bay Packers was voted the Most Valuable Player of Super Bowl II. It was his second Super Bowl MVP award.

■

Bill Miller snared two touchdown passes for the Oakland Raiders in Super Bowl II. Both catches were 23-yard touchdown receptions.

■

Green Bay Packers' head football coach Vince Lombardi retired from pro football after winning his second consecutive Super Bowl in 1968.

■

The Green Bay Packers won their second consecutive Super Bowl by beating the Oakland Raiders 33 to 14 in 1968.

SUPER BOWL III TIDBITS

Super Bowl III matched the New York Jets, the AFL champions, against the Baltimore Colts, the NFL champions.

∎

Three days before Super Bowl III, New York Jets quarterback Joe Namath publicly "guaranteed" a victory for his team over the Baltimore Colts.

∎

Weeb Ewbank, who coached the N.Y. Jets to a 16 to 7 victory over the Baltimore Colts in Super Bowl III, had formerly served as the head coach of the Baltimore Colts.

∎

The Baltimore Colts were coached by Don Shula in Super Bowl III.

The quarterback for the Baltimore Colts in Super Bowl III was Earl Morrall. Earl Morrall guided the Baltimore Colts to the NFL Championship and into Super Bowl III after replacing injured All-Pro QB Johnny Unitas during the regular season.

■

Quarterback Johnny Unitas came off of the bench and led the Baltimore Colts to the only touchdown they scored in Super Bowl III.

■

Key players for the New York Jets in their 1969 Super Bowl victory were running back Matt Snell, field goal kicker Jim Turner, defensive players Larry Grantham and Randy Beverly, and New York Jets QB Joe Namath, who was named the Most Valuable Player of Super Bowl III.

The Kansas City Chiefs upset the favored Minnesota Vikings 23 to 7 to capture Super Bowl IV.

■

Hank Stram of the Kansas City Chiefs was the winning coach in Super Bowl IV. Bud Grant of the Minnesota Vikings was the losing coach.

■

Defensive stars for the Minnesota Vikings in Super Bowl IV included linemen Jim Marshall and Carl Eller.

■

Defensive stars for the Kansas City Chiefs in Super Bowl IV included middle linebacker Willie Lanier and tackle Buck Buchanan.

■

Len Dawson, the quarterback of the Kansas City Chiefs, became the fourth QB in a row to be named the Super Bowl MVP when he won the award in 1970 for Super Bowl IV.

Super Bowl IV was the first Super Bowl played after the merger of the American Football League with the National Football League.

■

Super Bowl V pitted the Dallas Cowboys of the NFL's American Football Conference against the Baltimore Colts of the NFL's National Football Conference.

■

Coach Tom Landry of the Dallas Cowboys opposed Coach Don McCafferty of the Baltimore Colts in Super Bowl V.

Super Bowl V was the first Super Bowl to be played on artificial turf.

■

Johnny Unitas was the starting quarterback for the Baltimore Colts in Super Bowl V. When Unitas was injured in the contest, he was replaced by Earl Morrell.

■

Tight end John Mackey scored on a 75-yard touchdown pass from Baltimore Colts QB John Unitas in the second quarter of Super Bowl V.

■

The backfield for the Dallas Cowboys in Super Bowl V included quarterback Craig Morton and backs Calvin Hill, Walt Garrison, and Duane Thomas.

With five seconds remaining in Super Bowl V, Jim O'Brien of the Baltimore Colts kicked a 32-yard field goal to give the Colts a dramatic 16 to 13 win over the Dallas Cowboys. His game-winning field goal was set up by a key interception by Baltimore Colts' linebacker Mike Curtis.

■

Don McCafferty of the Baltimore Colts was the first rookie NFL coach to win a Super Bowl.

■

Linebacker Chuck Howley of the Dallas Cowboys was the first member of a losing team to be named the MVP of a Super Bowl. Howley's Dallas Cowboys lost to the Baltimore Colts in Super Bowl V.

■

The Dallas Cowboys returned to the Super Bowl in 1972 to play in their second consecutive Super Bowl Contest.

Super Bowl VI matched two pro football mentors against each other. Coach Tom Landry of the Dallas Cowboys matched gridiron wits with Don Shula of the Miami Dolphins in the 1972 Super Bowl.

■

The opposing quarterbacks in the 1972 Super Bowl were Bob Griese of the Miami Dolphins and Roger Staubach of the Dallas Cowboys.

■

The Dallas Cowboys defeated the Miami Dolphins 24 to 3 in Super Bowl VI.

■

The only time sure-handed running back Larry Csonka of the Miami Dolphins fumbled during the 1971 season was in Super Bowl VI. The ball was recovered by linebacker Chuck Howley and led to a Dallas field goal.

Super Bowl VI was the first time in Super Bowl history a defensive team did not give up a touchdown to an opponent. The Dallas Cowboys defense limited the Miami Dolphins to just 185 yards on offense and did not surrender a touchdown.

■

QB Roger Staubach earned the MVP award in Super Bowl VI by throwing touchdown passes to Lance Alworth and Mike Ditka in the game.

SUPER BOWL BRAINERS

See how you fare on these questions regarding Super Bowls:

1. Which two teams played in Super Bowl VII, and who won the game?

2. Who beat the Minnesota Vikings in Super Bowl VIII and what was the score of the game?

3. A defensive safety man was the MVP of Super Bowl VII. A running back was the Most Valuable Player of Super Bowl VIII. Can you name those MVP's?

4. Where were Super Bowls VII and VIII played?

Answers

1. The Washington Redskins played the Miami Dolphins on January 14, 1973 in Super Bowl VII. Miami won the game, beating Washington 14 to 7.

2. The Miami Dolphins beat the Minnesota Vikings 24 to 7 in Super Bowl VIII.

3. Defensive safety Jake Scott of the Miami Dolphins was the MVP of Super Bowl VII. Running back Larry Csonka of the Miami Dolphins was the Most Valuable Player of Super Bowl VIII.

4. Super Bowl VII was played in Los Angeles, California at the Memorial Bowl. VIII was played in Houston, Texas at Rice Stadium.

The Pittsburgh Steelers, led by quarterback Terry Bradshaw, beat the Minnesota Vikings 16 to 6 in Super Bowl IX, which took place in 1975.

■

In Super Bowl IX, the Minnesota Vikings became the first pro football team to lose three Super Bowls.

■

The first safety in a Super Bowl was scored in 1975. Defensive end Dwight White of the Pittsburgh Steelers, with help from linebacker Jack Lambert, downed Minnesota Vikings' quarterback Fran Tarkenton in the end zone to score two points for the Steelers.

■

Minnesota's Terry Brown recovered a blocked Pittsburgh Steelers punt in the end zone to tally the only points scored by the Vikings in their 16 to 6 loss in Super Bowl IX.

Franco Harris of the Pittsburgh Steelers set a record by rushing for 158 yards in Super Bowl IX. For his effort, Franco Harris was named the Most Valuable Player of the 1975 Super Bowl.

■

Franco Harris of the Pittsburgh Steelers is the all-time rushing leader in Super Bowl play. In four Super Bowl contests, Franco Harris rushed for a total of 354 yards.

■

The Pittsburgh Steelers edged the Dallas Cowboys 21 to 17 in Super Bowl X in 1976 to capture back-to-back Super Bowl titles.

■

Pittsburgh Steelers' Lynn Swann scored the deciding touchdown in Super Bowl X by catching a 64-yard T.D. toss from Steelers' quarterback Terry Bradshaw. Lynn Swann was named the game's Most Valuable Player.

Receiver Lynn Swann of the Pittsburgh Steelers played in four Super Bowls and caught sixteen passes for 364 yards and three T.D.'s.

■

The Cowboys' all-star receiver Drew Pearson scored the first points in Super Bowl X by catching a 29-yard T.D. toss from Dallas quarterback Roger Staubach.

■

A Super Bowl game was played in the Rose Bowl in Pasadena, California for the first time in history in 1977 in Super Bowl XI.

■

Super Bowl XI was the first time in history that over 100,000 fans attended a Super Bowl contest. The attendance for Super Bowl XI, which was played on January 9, 1977, was 103,438 people.

The opposing coaches in Super Bowl XI were John Madden of the Oakland Raiders and Bud Grant of the Minnesota Vikings.

■

Ken Stabler, the starting quarterback for the Oakland Raiders in Super Bowl XI, was a left-handed quarterback. He was the first left-handed QB to start a Super Bowl.

■

The Oakland Raiders used a potent passing attack to defeat the Minnesota Vikings by the score of 32 to 14 in Super Bowl XI.

■

Wide receiver Fred Biletnikoff of the Oakland Raiders caught four passes for 79 yards to win the MVP award in Super Bowl XI.

Oakland Raiders' cornerback Willie Brown intercepted a Minnesota Vikings' pass in the fourth quarter of Super Bowl XI and returned it 75 yards for a touchdown.

■

Bud Grant of the Minnesota Vikings became the first coach to lose four times in Super Bowl competition when his team was defeated by the Oakland Raiders in Super Bowl XI in 1977.

■

The Dallas Cowboys defeated the Denver Broncos in Super Bowl XII, which was played on January 15, 1978 in New Orleans at the Louisiana Superdome.

■

The quarterback for the Denver Broncos in Super Bowl XII was Craig Morton. Craig Morton played quarterback for the Dallas Cowboys in Super Bowl V in 1971.

Red Miller of the Denver Broncos was the losing coach in Super Bowl XII.

■

Q.B. Craig Morton of the Denver Broncos threw four interceptions in the 1978 Super Bowl.

■

The Super Bowl's Most Valuable Player Award was shared for the first time in 1978. Defensive linemen Harvey Martin and Randy White of the Dallas Cowboys were named co-MVP's of Super Bowl XII.

■

The Pittsburgh Steelers edged the Dallas Cowboys 35 to 31 to win Super Bowl XIII in 1979. The Pittsburgh Steelers became the first team in NFL history to win three Super Bowls.

QB Terry Bradshaw of the Pittsburgh Steelers passed for 300 yards in a single game for the first time in his NFL career in Super Bowl XIII. Bradshaw passed for 318 yards and 4 touchdowns against the Dallas Cowboys in the 1979 Super Bowl.

■

Linebacker Mike Hegman of the Dallas Cowboys returned a fumble 37 yards for a touchdown against the Pittsburgh Steelers in Super Bowl XIII.

■

Quarterback Roger Staubach of the Dallas Cowboys threw four touchdown passes in a losing cause against the Pittsburgh Steelers in Super Bowl XIII.

■

Quarterback Terry Bradshaw of the Pittsburgh Steelers was named the Most Valuable Player of Super Bowl XIII and Super Bowl XIV.

The Pittsburgh Steelers beat the Los Angeles Rams 31 to 19 in Super Bowl XIV in 1980. The game was played before a crowd of 103,985 people in the Rose Bowl in Pasadena, California.

■

Coach Chuck Noll of the Pittsburgh Steelers won his fourth Super Bowl in 1980.

■

Ray Malavasi of the Los Angeles Rams was the losing coach in Super Bowl XIV.

■

Vince Ferragamo, the starting quarterback for the Los Angeles Rams in Super Bowl XIV, was formerly a pre-medical student at the University of Nebraska.

■

The first NFL team to win back to back Super Bowl titles twice was the Pittsburgh Steelers. They did in 1975 and 1976 and in 1979 and 1980.

Larry Anderson of the Pittsburgh Steelers returned five kickoffs for 162 yards against the Los Angeles Rams in Super Bowl XIV.

■

The Oakland Raiders won their second Super Bowl game in 1981. The Raiders beat the Philadelphia Eagles 27 to 10 in Super Bowl XV.

■

Oakland's Tom Flores was the winning coach of Super Bowl XV. Flores was the first man to play in a Super Bowl and then to win a Super Bowl as a coach.

■

The losing coach in Super Bowl XV was Dick Vermeil of the Philadelphia Eagles.

Quarterback Jim Plunkett of the Oakland Raiders threw three touchdown passes in Super Bowl XV to earn the game's MVP award.

■

Kenny King of the Oakland Raiders made an 80-yard TD catch in the 1981 Super Bowl.

■

The Oakland Raiders were the first NFL wild card team to win a Super Bowl, doing it in 1981.

■

Wilbert Montgomery of the Philadelphia Eagles led all receivers in catches in Super Bowl XV. Montgomery caught six passes from QB Ron Jaworski for 91 yards.

Super Bowl XVI was played at the Pontiac Silverdome in Pontiac, Michigan on January 24, 1982.

■

The San Francisco 49ers edged the Cincinnati Bengals 26 to 21 to win Super Bowl XVI.

■

Bill Walsh coached the San Francisco 49ers to victory in Super Bowl XVI.

■

Super Bowl XVI was the first time in Super Bowl history that the team that gained the most yards from scrimmage in the game lost the contest. Cincinnati gained 356 yards in Super Bowl XVI while San Francisco gained 275 yards.

Ken Anderson of the Cincinnati Bengals was the losing quarterback in Super Bowl XVI and Forrest Gregg was the losing coach.

■

In 1981, Dan Ross of the Cincinnati Bengals set a Super Bowl record by catching 11 passes in a losing effort against the San Francisco 49ers in Super Bowl XVI.

■

San Francisco 49ers' QB Joe Montana completed 14 of 22 passes for 157 yards to win the Most Valuable Player award in Super Bowl XVI.

■

In 1983, coach Joe Gibbs' Washington Redskins beat coach Don Shula's Miami Dolphins 27 to 17 in Super Bowl XVII.

Don Shula lost Super Bowl games as the head coach of two different teams (the Baltimore Colts and Miami Dolphins).

■

Fulton Walker of the Miami Dolphins scored a touchdown on a 98-yard kickoff return in Super Bowl XVII.

■

Joe Theismann quarterbacked the Washington Redskins and David Woodley quarterbacked the Miami Dolphins when the two teams met in Super Bowl XVII.

■

The Most Valuable Player in Super Bowl XVII was Washington Redskins' running back John Riggins, who gained 166 yards and scored one touchdown in the gridiron contest.

The Oakland Raiders were known as the Los Angeles Raiders when they returned to the Super Bowl in 1984 for Super Bowl XVIII.

■

The Los Angeles Raiders were victorious over the Washington Redskins in Super Bowl XVIII. The score of the contest was Raiders 38 and Redskins 9.

■

Linebacker Jack Squirek of the Los Angeles Raiders intercepted a pass and ran it back for a touchdown in the Raiders' victory over the Washington Redskins in Super Bowl XVIII.

■

Marcus Allen, the Los Angeles Raiders' star running back, rushed for a total of 191 yards, including a 74-yard touchdown run, in Super Bowl XVIII. Allen was named the Most Valuable Player of the game for his efforts.

MORE SUPER BOWL BRAINERS

It's time to make some super choices.
See if you can guess the correct answers to
these Super Bowl questions.

1. Who was the second man to play in a Super Bowl and
then coach a team to a Super Bowl victory? Was it
(A) Tom Landry, (B) Mike Ditka, or (C) Bill Parcells?

2. Which team did the Chicago Bears beat in Super Bowl
XX? Was it (A) the Miami Dolphins, (B) the Denver
Broncos, or (C) the New England Patriots?

3. Which member of the Chicago Bears was the Most
Valuable Player of Super Bowl XX? Was it (A) Jim
McMahon, (B) William Perry, or (C) Richard Dent?

4. Who made the only touchdown the New England
Patriots scored in Super Bowl XX? Was it (A) Irving
Fryar, (B) Tony Collins, or (C) Craig James.

Answers

1. B. Mike Ditka played in the 1972 Super Bowl as a member of the Dallas Cowboys and coached the Chicago Bears to a Super Bowl victory in 1986.

2. C. The Chicago Bears defeated the New England Patriots in Super Bowl XX by the score of 46 to 10.

3. C. End Richard Dent, who helped the Bears' defense sack New England quarterback Steven Grogan seven times in the game, was named the MVP of Super Bowl XX.

4. A. Irving Fryer scored on an 8-yard touchdown pass thrown by quarterback Steven Grogan in Super Bowl XX.

The San Francisco 49ers topped the Miami Dolphins in Super Bowl XIX in 1985. San Francisco outscored Miami 38 to 16 in the game.

■

QB Joe Montana of the San Francisco 49ers completed 24 of 35 passes for 331 yards and three touchdowns in Super Bowl XIX. Montana was named the Most Valuable Player for the game.

■

Quarterback Jim McMahon of the Chicago Bears was the first quarterback to score two rushing touchdowns in a Super Bowl. In Super Bowl XX, in which New England beat Chicago 46 to 10, McMahon scored on runs of two yards and one yard.

■

Super Bowl XXI was won by the New York Giants. The Giants posted a 39 to 20 victory over the Denver Broncos in the 1987 Super Bowl.

The Most Valuable Player of Super Bowl XXI was New York Giants quarterback Phil Simms, who passed for 268 yards and three touchdowns.

■

QB Phil Simms of the New York Giants connected on ten straight completions in Super Bowl XXI.

■

When the New York Giants won the Super Bowl in 1987, they were coached by Bill Parcells, who is nicknamed the "Tuna."

■

After winning Super Bowl XXI in 1987, the New York Giants did not even make the NFL playoffs the following season.

■

The Denver Broncos lost their second straight Super Bowl in 1988. The Broncos lost to the Washington

Redskins by the score of 42 to 10 in Super Bowl XXII. Coach Dan Reeves of the Denver Broncos lost back-to-back Super Bowls in 1987 and 1988.

■

Super Bowl XXII was held at Jack Murphy Stadium in San Diego, California.

■

In 1988, Doug Williams of the Washington Redskins became the first African-American quarterback to start a Super Bowl. Williams was also named the Most Valuable Player of Super Bowl XXII.

■

The San Francisco 49ers won their third Super Bowl championship in 1989. Coach Bill Walsh's 49ers defeated Coach Sam Wyche's Cincinnati Bengals 20 to 16 in Super Bowl XXIII.

■

Receiver Jerry Rice of the San Francisco 49ers was named the MVP of Super Bowl XXIII for catching

11 passes for 215 yards and one touchdown.
Roger Craig of the San Francisco 49ers played in three Super Bowls. In his Super Bowl career, Roger Craig rushed for a total of 201 yards and two touchdowns and caught 20 passes for 212 yards and two touchdowns.

■

Stanford Jennings of the Cincinnati Bengals had a 93-yard kickoff return for a touchdown against the San Francisco 49ers in the 1989 Super Bowl.

■

New head coach George Seifert guided the San Francisco 49ers to their fourth Super Bowl victory in 1990 in Super Bowl XXIV.

■

In 1995, coach George Seifert of the San Francisco 49ers won his second Super Bowl title by defeating coach Bobby Ross' San Diego Chargers.

The San Francisco 49er's beat the Denver Broncos in Super Bowl XXIV by the score of 55 to 10. The 55 points scored by the San Francisco 49ers in Super Bowl XXIV were the most points ever scored in a Super Bowl contest.

■

QB Joe Montana was named the Most Valuable Player of the Super Bowl for a record third time in 1990.

■

Coach Bill Parcells led the New York Giants to a second Super Bowl crown in 1991 in Super Bowl XXV.

■

The New York Giants slipped by the Buffalo Bills by the score of 20 to 19 in Super Bowl XXV. It was the closest margin of victory ever in a Super Bowl contest.

When the New York Giants met the Buffalo (N.Y.) Bills in Super Bowl XXV, it was the first time a Super Bowl game matched two teams from the same state.

■

Running back Otis Anderson of the New York Giants was the MVP of Super Bowl XXV.

■

Marv Levy of the Buffalo Bills is the only NFL coach to lose four straight Super Bowls.

■

Quarterback Mark Rypien of the Washington Redskins was the MVP of Super Bowl XXVI.

■

The Washington Redskins beat the Buffalo Bills 37 to 24 in Super Bowl XXVI.

■

Troy Aikman, the quarterback of the Dallas Cowboys, was the Most Valuable Player of Super Bowl XXVII.

The Dallas Cowboys beat the Buffalo Bills 52 to 17 in Super Bowl XXVII.

■

Dallas Cowboys' running back Emmitt Smith was the MVP of Super Bowl XXVIII.

■

The Dallas Cowboys beat the Buffalo Bills 30 to 13 in Super Bowl XXVIII.

■

Coach Jimmy Johnson of the Dallas Cowboys won back-to-back Super Bowl titles in 1993 and 1994 (Super Bowls XXVII and XXVIII).

■

Quarterback Roger Staubach of the Dallas Cowboys played in four Super Bowls and passed for a Super Bowl total of 734 yards and eight touchdowns.

Quarterback Steve Young of the San Francisco 49ers was the Most Valuable Player of Super Bowl XXIX.

■

The San Francisco 49ers won a record fifth Super Bowl game when they beat the San Diego Chargers 49 to 26 in Super Bowl XXIX.

■

Andre Coleman of the San Diego Chargers returned a kickoff 98 yards for a touchdown against the San Francisco 49ers in Super Bowl XXIX.

■

Super Bowl XXIX was the second time two teams from the same state (San Francisco, California and San Diego, California) met for the championship.

■

The Super Bowl was played at Sun Devil Stadium in Tempe, Arizona for the first time in 1996 for Super Bowl XXX.

The Pittsburgh Steelers lost to the Dallas Cowboys in Super Bowl XXX by the score of 27 to 17.

■

Barry Switzer of the Dallas Cowboys was the winning coach in Super Bowl XXX, and Bill Cowher of the Pittsburgh Steelers was the losing coach.

■

Cornerback Larry Brown of the Dallas Cowboys had two interceptions in Super Bowl XXX and was named the Most Valuable Player of the game.

■

The Green Bay Packers, coached by Mike Holmgren, won Super Bowl XXXI by beating the New England Patriots, coached by Bill Parcells, 31 to 24.

■

In Super Bowl XXXI, Desmond Howard of Green Bay returned a kickoff 99 yards. Howard, who had 244 total return yards, won the MVP trophy.

Super Bowl XXXI was the Packers' first Super Bowl win in 29 years.

■

Antonio Freeman of the Green Bay Packers played in two Super Bowls, including Super Bowl XXXI, and caught 12 passes for 231 yards and three touchdowns.

■

Coach Mike Shanahan's Denver Broncos captured back-to-back Super Bowl titles winning games in 1998 and 1999. The Denver Broncos beat the Green Bay Packers 31 to 24 in Super Bowl XXXII. They also beat the Atlanta Falcons 34 to 19 in Super Bowl XXXIII.

■

Running back Terrell Davis of the Denver Broncos was the Most Valuable Player of Super Bowl XXXII. Davis gained 157 yards and scored three touchdowns in the 1998 Super Bowl.

When the Denver Broncos beat the Atlanta Falcons in Super Bowl XXXIII, Falcon's coach Dan Reeves became the second coach to lose four Super Bowl games. Coach Reeves had previously lost the Super Bowl three times earlier as the head coach of the Denver Broncos.

■

Quarterback John Elway of the Denver Broncos, who was the MVP of Super Bowl XXXIII, rushed for four touchdowns in his five game Super Bowl career.

■

The St. Louis Rams defeated the Tennessee Titans 23 to 16 in Super Bowl XXXIV.

■

Mike Jones of the St. Louis Rams tackled ballcarrier Kevin Dyson of the Tennessee Titans at the one-yard line on the final play of Super Bowl XXXIV to preserve a Super Bowl win for the Rams.

The winning coach of Super Bowl XXXIV was Dick Vermeil of the St. Louis Rams. Kurt Warner, the quarterback for the St. Louis Rams in Super Bowl XXXIV, was voted the game's Most Valuable Player. Warner completed 24 or 45 passes for 414 yards and two touchdowns in the 2000 Super Bowl.

■

Super Bowl XXXV, played in 2001, was won by the Baltimore Ravens, who beat the N.Y. Giants 34 to 7.

■

Brian Billick was head coach of the Baltimore Ravens when they won Super Bowl XXXV.

■

Linebacker Ray Lewis of the Baltimore Ravens was the MVP of Super Bowl XXXV.

Coach Bill Belichick's New England Patriots beat coach Mike Martz's St. Louis Rams 20 to 17 in Super Bowl XXXVI.

■

Super Bowl XXXVI was played on February 3, 2002 at the Louisiana Superdome in New Orleans, Louisiana. It was the first Super Bowl contest ever played in February.

■

New England Patriots quarterback Tom Brady was the MVP of Super Bowl XXXVI.

■

The Tampa Bay Buccaneers won Super Bowl XXXVII by defeating the Oakland Raiders 48 to 21.

■

Safety Dexter Jackson of the Tampa Bay Buccaneers had two interceptions in the 2003 Super Bowl and was named the MVP of the game.

Jon Gruden of the Tampa Bay Buccaneers was the winning coach in Super Bowl XXXVII.

■

The Carolina Panthers went to Super Bowl XXXVIII after posting dismal regular season records of 1 win and 15 losses in 2001 and 7 wins and 9 losses in 2002.

■

The New England Patriots won Super Bowl XXXVIII by beating the Carolina Panthers 32 to 29.

■

Kicker Adam Vinatieri of the New England Patriots booted the game-winning field goal against the Carolina Panthers in Super Bowl XXXVIII with only four seconds remaining in the championship contest.

■

Quarterback Tom Brady of the New England Patriots won his second Super Bowl MVP award in 2004.

The New England Patriots beat the Philadelphia Eagles at Alltel Stadium, in Jacksonville, Florida in Super Bowl XXXIX by a score of 24 to 21. That made New England winners of two Super Bowls in a row, and three in the last four years, earning them the title "The first twenty-first century dynasty."

■

In Super Bowl XXXIX, wideout Deion Branch caught 11 passes for 133 yards, tying a Super Bowl record for number of catches. He was named MVP of the Super Bowl.

■

The coach of the New England Patriots in Super Bowl XXXIX was Bill Belichick. New England's victory put him among the coach leaders, giving him three Super Bowl victories. Only Chuck Noll (four), Bill Walsh (three), and Joe Gibbs (three) have as many.

CHAPTER 6

TAKE A HIKE, QUARTERBACK

Quarterback Brett Favre takes the snap from center. Signal-caller Donovan McNabb backpedals into the pocket. QB Matt Hasselbeck looks downfield for a receiver. Field general David Carr prepares to fire the pigskin. Team leader Peyton Manning launches a long bomb. Quarterback Dante Culpepper completes the pass. It's another touchdown toss for QB Rich Gannon.

No matter who your favorite college or pro quarterback is, there's no doubting that the QB is a football team's most important player. If you're a fan of famous and fearless quarterbacks, get ready to pass the time reading about some of the gridiron's greatest signal-callers.

Rich Gannon of the Oakland Raiders was voted the quarterback of the 2002 All-NFL team.

■

Notre Dame quarterback Paul Hornung is the only man to ever win the Heisman Trophy while playing for a college team with a losing record. Hornung won college football's top award in 1956 while playing for a Notre Dame team that won only two games and lost eight.

■

The Indianapolis Colts retired the jersey number of quarterback Johnny Unitas. Johnny Unitas wore No. 19.

■

Jim Kelly passed for 35,467 yards in his 11 seasons as a pro quarterback for the Buffalo Bills.

Danny Wuerffel of Florida won the Davy O'Brien National Quarterback Award as America's top college QB in 1995 and in 1996. He also won the Heisman Trophy in 1996.

■

On October 28, 1962, quarterback Y.A. Tittle of the New York Giants passed for 505 yards in a game against the Washington Redskins.

■

An unwritten rule in football is that nobody speaks in the offensive huddle except the quarterback.

■

On November 19, 1961 quarterback George Blanda of the Houston Oilers threw seven touchdown passes in a game against the New York Titans.

■

Terry Bradshaw once started 56 straight games at quarterback for the Pittsburgh Steelers.

A quarterback sneak is a tricky running play where the center snaps the ball to the QB, who then immediately rushes forward behind the block of the center.

■

While at Brigham Young University, quarterback Jim McMahon passed for 342 yards in a single half of a football game. The game was against Utah State on October 18, 1980 and BYU won the contest 70 to 46.

■

Quarterback Steve Young of the San Francisco 49ers led the NFC in passing six out of seven years from 1991 to 1997.

■

In 1995, Brett Favre of the Green Bay Packers led the NFC in passing with 359 completions for 4,413 yards and 38 touchdowns.

■

Quarterback David Carr of Fresno State was the first player taken in the 2002 NFL draft. Carr was selected by the Houston Texans.

MANNING THE QB POSITION

Quarterback Archie Manning was the number one draft pick of the New Orleans Saints in the 1971 NFL Draft. He also played for the Houston Oilers and the Minnesota Vikings.

During his NFL career, QB Archie Manning completed 2,011 of 3,642 passes for 23,911 yards and 125 touchdowns.

Archie Manning's sons Peyton and Eli are quarterbacks who were both number one picks in the NFL draft.

QB Peyton Manning of the Indianapolis Colts led the AFC in passing in 1999.

Eli Manning was a rookie quarterback for the N.Y. Giants in 2004. On Manning's first regular season play, he handed the ball off to running back Tiki Barber, who scampered for a 72-yard touchdown run.

Super Bowl champion quarterback Tom Brady of the New England Patriots did not start a single game for his high school freshman football team in California even though his team was 0-9.

■

Jim Plunkett, Joe Kapp, and Tom Flores are all Mexican-American athletes who played quarterback in the National Football League.

■

Sonny Sixkiller is a Native American athlete who established numerous passing records in the 1970's as a quarterback at the University of Washington.

■

Los Angeles Rams' star quarterback Roman Gabriel is the son of a Filipino laborer who immigrated to the United States.

George Blanda was intercepted more times than any other NFL quarterback. Blanda threw 277 interceptions during his long NFL career.

■

Joe Namath of the N.Y. Jets was the first NFL quarterback to pass for more than 4,000 yards in a single season. Namath passed for 4,007 yards in 1967.

■

Quarterback Ty Detmer attempted 1,530 passes during his college career at Brigham Young University. He completed 958 of those passes.

■

Quarterback Willie Totten of I-AA Mississippi Valley threw nine touchdown passes in a game against Kentucky State in 1984.

YOUR NUMBER IS UP

All of the following quarterbacks have had their jersey numbers retired by their respective pro teams. Can you match the QBs with their correct jersey numbers? Complete the task and you pass.

1. Joe Namath (N.Y. Jets)   A. No. 16
2. Steve Grogan (N.E. Patriots)   B. No. 12
3. Len Dawson (K.C. Chiefs)   C. No. 14

The answers are: 1.(B) The New York Jets retired Joe Namath's No. 12. 2.(C) The New England Patriots retired Steve Grogan's No. 14. 3.(A) The Kansas City Chiefs retired Len Dawson's No. 16.

Quarterback Daryle Lamonica of the Oakland Raiders was the last man to be named the Most Valuable Player of the American Football League. Lamonica won the award in 1967. In 1970, the AFL merged with the NFL and became the AFC.

■

On September 28, 1951, quarterback Norm Van Brocklin of the Los Angeles Rams passed for 555 yards in a NFL game against the New York Giants.

■

Former Dallas Cowboy quarterback Danny White was a head coach in the Arena Football League in 2003.

■

Quarterback Stacey Robinson of Northern Illinois rushed for 308 yards and five T.D.'s in a 73 to 18 victory over Fresno State on October 6, 1990.

Quarterback Khari Jones of the Winnipeg Blue Bombers was named the Most Outstanding Player in the Canadian Football League in 2001.

■

Quarterback Doug Flutie was named the Most Outstanding Player in the Canadian Football League six out of seven years from 1991 to 1997 while playing for three different CFL teams (B.C. Lions, Calgary Stampeders, and Toronto Argonauts).

■

In 1944, Angelo Bertelli of Notre Dame became the first quarterback ever to be selected as a number one pick in the NFL Draft. Bertelli was selected by the Boston Yanks.

In 1948, the Chicago Bears had three future Hall of Fame quarterbacks on their team roster. The Bears' first- and third-string quarterbacks were Sid Luckman and Bobby Layne, who were later voted into the Pro Football Hall of Fame. The second-string quarterback was Johnny Lujack, who was later voted into the College Football Hall of Fame.

BOB WATERFIELD TIDBITS

Quarterback Bob Waterfield of the Los Angeles Rams was also an outstanding field goal kicker and punter. He booted 60 field goals and kicked 315 extra points during his NFL career.

During his NFL career, QB Bob Waterfield passed for 98 touchdowns and scored 13 rushing touchdowns.

Bob Waterfield had a 42.4 yard average as a punter and was credited with two 88-yard punts during his pro career.

In addition to playing quarterback and kicking for the L.A. Rams, Bob Waterfield also played defensive safety for five seasons and made 20 interceptions.

Drew Pearson, the famous Dallas Cowboys wide receiver, played quarterback at South River High School in New Jersey. Pearson started out as the backup signal-caller to quarterback Joe Theismann, who went on to play quarterback in the NFL for the Washington Redskins.

■

In 15 seasons as a NFL quarterback, Sonny Jurgensen of the Philadelphia Eagles and the Washington Redskins passed for 32,224 yards and 255 touchdowns.

■

John Brodie played quarterback for the San Francisco 49ers from 1957 to 1971. His best year was 1965, when he threw 30 touchdown passes.

■

On October 6, 1985, QB Joe Montana of the San Francisco 49ers set an NFL record by attempting 57 passes without an interception in a 38 to 17 win over the Atlanta Falcons.

Bobby Douglass of the Chicago Bears rushed for 968 yards as a quarterback during the 1972 NFL season.

∎

Quarterback Ed Danowski of the New York Giants led the NFL in passing twice. In 1935, Danowski led the league by passing for 794 yards. In 1936, Ed Danowski passed for 848 yards, which was tops in the NFL.

∎

In 1989, QB Don Majkowski of the Green Bay Packers led the NFC in passing by completing 353 passes for 4,318 yards and 27 touchdowns.

Quarterback Ron Jaworski of the Philadelphia Eagles led the NFC in passing in 1980 by completing 257 passes for 3,529 yards and 27 touchdowns.

∎

The longest touchdown pass in the NFL during the 2002 regular season was a 99-yard T.D. toss from QB Trent Green of the Kansas City Chiefs to teammate Marc Boerigter. The touchdown play took place on December 22, 2002 against the San Diego Chargers.

∎

Quarterback Ken Anderson of the Cincinnati Bengals led the AFC in passing in 1982. Anderson completed 218 passes for 2,495 yards and 12 touchdowns.

∎

QB Boomer Esiason of the Cincinnati Bengals led the AFC in passing in 1988. Esiason threw for 3,572 yards and 28 touchdowns.

In 1984, quarterback Dan Marino of the Miami Dolphins passed for 48 touchdowns in a single NFL season.

■

No NFL quarterback threw 30 or more touchdown passes during the 2002 regular season.

■

Quarterback Joe Theismann of the Washington Redskins was named Pro Football's Offensive Player of the Year in 1983 by the Associated Press.

■

Quarterback Joe Kapp led the Minnesota Vikings to the NFL championship in 1969.

■

The first college football player ever drafted by the New York Jets was quarterback George Izo of Notre Dame, who was selected in 1960.

■

San Diego State quarterback Dennis Shaw tossed 9 touchdowns in a game against New Mexico State on November 15, 1969.

Quarterback Bill Anderson of Tulsa completed 42 of 65 passes in a game against Southern Illinois on October 30, 1965.

■

Quarterback Roman Gabriel of North Carolina State was the first player picked in the 1962 Pro Football draft. He was selected by the Oakland Raiders.

■

QB Matt Hasselbeck of the Seattle Seahawks completed 267 passes for 3,075 yards and 15 touchdowns in the 2002 NFL season.

■

Minnesota Vikings quarterback Daunte Culpepper threw a career high five touchdown passes in the Vikings' 35 to 17 opening day win over the Dallas Cowboys in 2004.

■

Quarterback Neil Lomax of the Arizona Cardinals passed for 4,614 yards during the 1984 NFL season.

A quarterback draw is a trick offensive play designed to confuse the defense. The quarterback takes the snap and drops back as if to pass the ball. As defenders rush toward him, the quarterback quickly pulls down the ball and runs forward with it past would-be tacklers.

■

Quarterback Warren Moon set a Minnesota Vikings team record when he passed for 4,264 yards in the 1994 NFL season.

■

The St. Louis Cardinals' team record of 154 touchdown passes in a career is held by signal-caller Roman Gabriel.

■

Miami Dolphins' quarterback Dan Marino threw a NFL record 352 touchdown passes in his career.

■

Quarterback Phil Simms passed for 199 touchdowns during his career, which is a N.Y. Giants' team record.

While playing quarterback for the Baltimore Colts, Bert Jones completed 17 passes in a row against the New York Jets on December 15, 1974.

■

QB Donovan McNabb passed for 330 yards and tied a career-high mark by completing four touchdown passes in the Philadelphia Eagles 31 to 17 win over the N.Y. Giants on opening day of the 2004 NFL season.

■

On September 15, 2002 quarterback Rich Gannon of the Oakland Raiders completed 43 of 63 passes for 403 yards and a touchdown in a game against the Pittsburgh Steelers.

■

NFL quarterback Brian Sipe holds the Cleveland Browns career records for the most passing yards (23,713) and the most touchdown passes (154).

EDDIE LEBARON TIDBITS

Eddie LeBaron was probably the smallest quarterback to ever play in the NFL. LeBaron, who played for the Washington Redskins and the Dallas Cowboys in the late 1950's and early 1960's, stood only 5 feet 5 inches tall and weighed less than 150 pounds.

■

Eddie LeBaron was so small he was nicknamed "The Little General."

■

During his 11-year NFL career, Eddie LeBaron passed for 13,330 yards.

■

Eddie LeBaron played for legendary coach Amos Alonzo Stagg at the College of the Pacific.

■

Eddie LeBaron was inducted into the College Football Hall of Fame in 1980.

Boomer Esiason was a left-handed quarterback who starred at the University of Maryland. He went on to play for the Cincinnati Bengals and the New York Jets.

■

Quarterbacks Tom Flores and Daryle Lamonica share the Oakland Raiders' team record for the most touchdown passes in a single game. Flores passed for six T.D.'s in a game in 1963 and Lamonica passed for six T.D.'s in a game in 1969.

■

In 2003, veteran QB Doug Flutie of the San Diego Chargers rushed for two touchdowns in the Chargers' 42-28 win over the Minnesota Vikings. Flutie became the first 40-year old quarterback to ever score a pair of rushing T.D.'s in a single NFL game.

■

Including his stints as a quarterback in the Canadian Football League and in the U.S. Football League, NFL veteran Doug Flutie has passed for over 50,000 yards in his pro career.

As a quarterback for the Seattle Seahawks, Dave Krieg threw five touchdown passes in one game three times during his career (1984, 1985, and 1988).

■

Rich Gannon of the Oakland Raiders completed more passes than any other NFL quarterback in 2002. Gannon completed 418 of 618 passes that season.

■

QB Roger Staubach of the Dallas Cowboys was nicknamed "Roger the Dodger" because of his ability to make tacklers miss him.

■

Quarterback Len Dawson spent five seasons in the NFL with the Pittsburgh Steelers and the Cleveland Browns before jumping to the American Football League to play for the Kansas City Chiefs.

■

Marcus Allen, the great NFL running back, was a quarterback and defensive back while in high school in California.

Quarterback Troy Aikman of UCLA was the first pick of the Dallas Cowboys in the 1989 NFL draft.

■

Atlanta Falcons' coach Dan Henning once made this comment about the passing of his starting quarterback David Archer. Said coach Henning, "They ought to send David to Washington. He can overthrow any government."

■

When he was a quarterback with the Pittsburgh Steelers, current TV sports analyst Terry Bradshaw described his running style this way. Said Bradshaw, "I'm a cross between a fullback and a sissy."

■

Detroit Lions quarterback Bobby Layne never admitted to defeat. Said Layne, "I never lost a game. I just ran out of time."

CHAPTER 7

CATCH PHRASES

How important are talented pass catchers to a football team? Head coach Bill Walsh of the NFL's San Francisco 49ers once summed up the answer to that question. Coach Walsh said, "If a team has a good quarterback and a good offensive line, can you win with mediocre receivers? I don't think so!"

If that's the case, don't let the chance to read about college and pro football's best receivers and receptions slip through your fingers. Catch up on your football reading and move on to this eye-catching chapter about some of the gridiron's greatest pigskin grabs.

A pass pattern is a special set manner in which a receiver runs and maneuvers in an attempt to position himself to catch the football.

■

In his first game as a member of the Philadelphia Eagles, wide receiver Terrell Owens caught three touchdown passes in a 31 to 17 opening day win over the New York Giants on September 12, 2004.

■

Todd Christensen set a team record for the Oakland Raiders in 1986 when he caught 95 passes in a single season.

■

Fred Arbanas of the Kansas City Chiefs was named the tight end on the All-Time American Football League team.

Charley Taylor of the Washington Redskins caught 649 passes during his NFL career, which lasted from 1964 to 1977.

■

Elroy Hirsch is considered to be pro football's first flanker. As a member of the Los Angeles Rams in 1949, halfback Hirsch was often split out to act as an extra receiver in the Rams' new style passing attack.

■

Flanker back Elroy Hirsch is best remembered by his famous nickname "Crazy Legs." Elroy "Crazy Legs" Hirsch had his own unique style of running.

■

A slant pass is a quickly thrown ball to a receiver who swiftly cuts across the middle of the field on a sharp angle.

■

Jay Miller of BYU was the first Division One college receiver to make 100 catches in a single season. Miller made 100 catches in 1973 to lead all college receivers that year.

Wide receiver Lance Alworth of the San Diego Chargers was the first former American Football League player elected to the Pro Football Hall of Fame.

■

A post pattern is when a receiver runs straight down the field for a specific distance and then cuts on an angle toward the goalpost in the middle of the field.

■

In 1968, Ron Sellers of Florida State led all college receivers in passes caught by making 86 receptions for 1,496 yards and 12 T.D.'s.

■

The NFL passed a rule in 1946 that made a forward pass automatically incomplete if it struck the goalpost.

■

In 1934, Joe Carter of the Philadelphia Eagles and Morris "Red" Badgro of the N.Y. Giants shared the NFL pass catching title. Carter and Badgro caught a mere 16 passes each that season.

A buttonhook or hook pattern is when a receiver runs straight down the field for a specific distance and then makes a sharp U-turn to face the quarterback, who instantly throws him the ball.

■

Ryan Yarborough of Wyoming caught 229 passes that were good for 4,357 yards during his college football career, which lasted from 1990 to 1993.

■

Wyoming receiver Marcus Harris played college football from 1993 to 1996 and caught 259 passes for a total of 4,518 yards.

■

Wide receiver Bob Hayes of the Dallas Cowboys won a gold medal in the 400-meter relay at the 1964 Olympic Games. Hayes snared 365 passes for 7,295 yards during his NFL career.

■

Wide receiver Tim Brown of Notre Dame won the Heisman Trophy in 1987.

Johnny Rogers of Nebraska was the first flanker to ever win the Heisman Trophy as college football's top player. Rogers won the award in 1972.

■

Michigan's Charles Woodson, who played both wide receiver and defensive back, won college football's Heisman Trophy in 1997.

FAME GAMERS

Can you successfully complete the quiz below by matching the following famous pass receivers with the correct year each one was elected to the Pro Football Hall of Fame?

1. Lance Alworth   A. 1983
(San Diego Chargers)

2. Paul Warfield   B. 1987
(Cleveland Browns)

3. Don Maynard   C. 1978
(New York Jets)

4. John Stallworth   D. 2002
(Pittsburgh Steelers)

The correct connections are 1-C (Lance Alworth in 1978), 2-A (Paul Warfield in 1983), 3-B (Don Maynard in 1987), and 4-D (John Stallworth in 2002).

Charlie Hennigan of the Houston Oilers caught 101 passes during the 1964 NFL season.

■

Receiver Andre Reed caught 700 passes for 9,848 yards during his NFL career with the Buffalo Bills.

■

Ray Flaherty of the N.Y. Giants led the NFL in pass catches in 1932 with only 21 receptions.

■

The wide receivers selected to the 2002 All-Canadian Football League squad were Derick Armstrong of the Saskatchewan Roughriders and Jason Tucker of the Edmonton Eskimos.

■

Stanley Morgan caught 534 passes and scored 68 touchdowns as a member of the New England Patriots from 1977 to 1989.

■

Randy Gatewood of UNLV (the University of Nevada at Las Vegas) caught 23 passes in a game against Idaho in 1994.

THE IMMACULATE RECEPTION

The Immaculate Reception was one of the most famous catches ever made in the history of the NFL. It occurred during a playoff game between the Pittsburgh Steelers and the Oakland Raiders on December 23, 1972. Oakland was leading Pittsburgh by the score of 7 to 6 with only 22 seconds remaining in the contest. It was fourth down and ten at the Pittsburgh 40-yard line. Steelers' quarterback Terry Bradshaw threw a pass to teammate "Frenchy" Fuqua. Defensive back Jack Tatum of the Raiders deflected the pass up into the air. Pittsburgh fullback Franco Harris came out of nowhere to make a shoestring catch of the deflected pass. Harris then rumbled 60 yards with the ball for a touchdown to give the Pittsburgh Steelers a playoff victory. The amazing play has been known as "The Immaculate Reception" ever since.

A flare pass is a short pass to a player swinging wide or flaring out of the backfield. A flare pass is usually thrown to a running back.

■

Baltimore Colts' wide receiver Raymond Berry snared 631 passes for 9,275 yards during his NFL career.

■

Ray Perkins, who was an NFL player and coach, was an All-American wide receiver at the University of Alabama. While at Alabama, Perkins caught passes thrown by future NFL star quarterbacks Joe Namath (N.Y. Jets) and Ken Stabler (Oakland Raiders).

■

Tom Fears of the Los Angeles Rams caught 18 passes in one game in a contest against the Green Bay Packers in 1950.

■

Oakland Raiders' wide receiver Fred Biletnikoff led all NFL receivers with 61 catches in 1971.

Steve Largent caught 819 passes during his NFL career with the Seattle Seahawks.

■

Cris Carter caught 122 passes in 1994 and 122 passes in 1995 as a receiver for the Minnesota Vikings.

■

Art Monk pulled in 888 passes as a receiver for the Washington Redskins from 1980 to 1993.

Don Hutson, a receiver for the Green Bay Packers, led the NFL in scoring five straight years from 1940 to 1944.

■

Green Bay Packers' receiver Don Hutson was the first player in NFL history to score over 100 points in a single season. In 1942, Hutson tallied 138 points to lead all NFL scorers.

■

Drew Pearson of the Dallas Cowboys led the NFL in catches in 1976. Pearson caught 58 passes for 806 yards and 6 T.D.'s that season.

■

NFL sportscaster Cris Collinsworth caught 417 passes in his career as a wide receiver for the Cincinnati Bengals.

■

Wide receiver Jerry Rice caught 301 passes during his college football career at Mississippi Valley State University.

■

End Dante Lavelli, who played for the Cleveland Browns in the 1940's, was nicknamed "Glue Fingers" because of his uncanny ability to catch the football.

In college football, if a receiver jumps in the air to catch a pass along the sidelines and has possession and control of the ball when he lands with only one foot inbounds, the catch is good.

■

In pro football, if a receiver jumps into the air to make a catch along the sidelines he must land with both feet inbounds in order for the catch to be good. The only exception is if a defender forces the receiver out of bounds before his feet can touch down.

■

Pete Pihos of the Philadelphia Eagles led the NFL in pass receptions in 1953 (63 receptions) and in 1955 (62 receptions). In 1954, Pihos shared the NFL pass-catching crown with Billy Wilson of the San Francisco 49ers (60 receptions each).

■

Michael Irvin of the Dallas Cowboys caught 111 passes for 1,603 yards during the 1995 season.

End Waddy Young was the first player from the University of Oklahoma to be named an All-American (1938). He died in WWII when his B-29 bomber crashed during the first U.S. bombing raid on Tokyo, Japan.

■

Randy Moss of the Minnesota Vikings led the NFC in receiving in 2002 with 106 catches.

■

Marvin Harrison of the Indianapolis Colts led the AFC in receiving in 2002 with 143 catches.

■

Milt Stegall of the Winnipeg Blue Bombers led the Canadian Football League in receiving in 2002 with 106 catches for 1,896 yards and 23 touchdowns.

■

Tight ends Dave Casper, John Mackey, and Kellen Winslow are all members of the Pro Football Hall of Fame.

Oakland Raiders' (and former San Francisco 49ers') wide receiver Jerry Rice's streak of 274 straight games with at least one catch ended on September 19, 2004 when the Raiders beat the Buffalo Bills 13 to 10.

■

Arnold Jackson caught 300 passes playing college football for Louisville from 1997 to 2000.

■

John Stallworth hauled in 537 passes as a receiver for the Pittsburgh Steelers from 1974 to 1987.

■

Bill Hewitt was an All-Pro end for the Chicago Bears in 1933. Hewitt was known for playing without a helmet before NFL rules required head gear.

■

Frank Hinkey was an All-American end at Yale from 1891 to 1893.

Split end Bill Carpenter of the 1958 Army football team became famous as the "Lonely End" of Coach Red Blaik's offensive scheme. "Lonely End" Bill Carpenter never came into the offensive huddle. The West Point receiver stayed split out all of the time. The Army quarterback told Carpenter which plays to run by using hand signals.

■

New York Giants' receiver Red Badgro was the first man to score a touchdown in a NFL championship game. Badgro caught a 29-yard touchdown toss against the Chicago Bears in the 1933 NFL title game.

■

Tight end Mike Ditka of the Chicago Bears was the NFL's Rookie of the Year in 1961. Ditka caught 56 passes for 1,076 yards and 12 T.D.'s his first year as a pro player.

CHAPTER 8

ON THE DEFENSIVE

A strong fence can keep unwanted visitors away from your property. A strong defense can prevent an opposing football squad from moving into your territory. So, football fans, get ready for some aggressive defensive work. Now is not the time to hold that line. Now is the time to rush forward and read lots of lines about charging defensive linemen, lightning-fast middle linebackers, and hard-hitting defensive backs.

There's the whistle. Let's break the huddle and tackle the tough guys of the gridiron—the Defense!

It is believed that defensive back Willie Brown of the Denver Broncos and Oakland Raiders invented the "bump and run" style of pass defense in which the defensive player bumps the receiver near the line of scrimmage to knock him off stride and delay his route, and then runs with him as he tries to complete the route.

■

A prevent defense is a defense specifically designed to stop long passes from being completed. It usually involves using extra defensive backs and fewer defensive linemen.

Defensive back Ronnie Lott was the first round draft pick of the San Francisco 49ers in the 1981 NFL draft.

■

Athletic director and football coach Pat Dye of Auburn University played linebacker for the Edmonton Eskimos of the Canadian Football League in the 1960's.

■

The front four of a defense are the defensive tackles and defensive ends.

■

Sports broadcaster Frank Gifford is best known as an offensive halfback for the New York Giants. However, when Frank Gifford first joined the N.Y. Giants in 1952, he was used primarily as a defensive back.

Dick Butkus was an All-American middle linebacker at the University of Illinois in 1963 and 1964.

■

Defensive lineman Richard Dent of the Chicago Bears led the National Football League with 17 quarterback sacks in 1985. He sacked opposing quarterbacks 137½ times in his 15-year NFL career.

■

Art Donovan was an All-Pro defensive tackle for the Baltimore Colts from 1954 to 1957.

■

In football, a player who tackles or downs an opposing ballcarrier in his own end zone scores a safety. A safety is worth two points.

Defensive back Barry Walker of the Detroit Lions returned a blocked field goal 92 yards for a touchdown in the Lions' 20 to 26 victory over the Chicago Bears on opening day of the 2004 NFL season.

■

An interception is when a defensive player catches a pass thrown to an offensive player.

Sam Huff was an All-Pro middle linebacker for the New York Giants in 1958 and 1959.

■

Linebacker Sam Huff intercepted 30 passes in his NFL career and returned two of them for touchdowns. Huff also returned three recovered fumbles for touchdowns.

■

Al Brosky of Illinois intercepted 29 passes during his NCAA-1A college football career.

■

On October 10, 2004 defensive end Julius Peppers of the Carolina Panthers intercepted a pass in the end zone against the Denver Broncos and ran the ball back 101 yards to the three-yard line. It was the longest interception return not to result in a touchdown in NFL history.

Ken Houston returned nine interceptions for touchdowns during his NFL career as a strong safety for the Houston Oilers.

■

A safety is a defensive back who plays in the middle of the field.

■

Safety Paul Krause of the Washington Redskins intercepted 81 passes during his 16-year NFL career.

■

Famous football coach Lou Holtz was a backup linebacker in his playing days at Kent State University.

■

Defensive lineman David "Deacon" Jones of the L.A. Rams coined the football term "Sack" for the tackle of an opposing quarterback attempting to pass.

A nose tackle is a defensive tackle who plays opposite an offensive center.

■

Nose tackle Cortez Kennedy of the Seattle Seahawks had 14 quarterback sacks in 1991.

■

In a 1969 poll of American sportswriters, Dick "Night Train" Lane of the Los Angeles Rams was selected as the best cornerback in the first 50 years of the NFL. Lane made 68 interceptions during his 14-year NFL career.

■

A cornerback is a defensive back who plays near the sidelines of the field. Cornerbacks are usually very agile athletes who can run fast.

■

Defensive tackle Alan Page of the Minnesota Vikings was the first defensive player to be named the Most Valuable Player of the NFL. Page was the MVP of the National Football League in 1971.

TEAMWORK

James Willis and Troy Vincent of the Philadelphia Eagles share the NFL record for the longest interception returned for a touchdown in an odd way. In a game against the Dallas Cowboys on November 3, 1996, James Willis intercepted a Dallas pass four yards deep in the end zone. Willis ran the ball out, returning it 14 yards. As James Willis was being brought down, he lateraled the pigskin to teammate Troy Vincent. Troy Vincent of the Philadelphia Eagles then returned the ball 90 yards for a T.D. Together Willis and Vincent combined to run back the interception 104 yards for a touchdown.

Defensive tackle Mike Reid of Penn State won the Outland Award as the Most Outstanding Interior Lineman in college football in 1969, the year college football celebrated its centennial.

■

Rashean Mathis of Bethune-Cookman intercepted 31 passes during his NCAA-1AA college football career.

■

Defensive lineman Deacon Jones of the Los Angeles Rams missed only three games in his 14-year NFL career.

■

Terrence Newman of Kansas State won the Thorpe Award as College Football's Most Outstanding Defensive Back in 2002.

■

In the 1970's and 1980's, the defensive team of the Minnesota Vikings was known as "The Purple People Eaters" (the color of the Vikings' jersey is purple).

Rocky Calmus of Oklahoma won the Butkus Award as College Football's Most Outstanding Linebacker in 2001.

■

Leon Hart of the Detroit Lions was named All-Pro as an offensive end by the Associated Press in 1951 and All-Pro at defensive end by United Press International that same year.

■

Linebacker Joe Schmidt was team captain of the Detroit Lions for nine years.

■

Star NFL lineman Bruce Smith won the Outland Trophy as College Football's Most Outstanding Interior Lineman in 1984 when he was a defensive tackle at Virginia Tech.

WHOOPS! WRONG WAY!

One of the most famous wrong-way runs in football history occurred in 1961 in a pro football game between the Minnesota Vikings and the San Francisco 49ers. Defensive end Jim Marshall of the Vikings scooped up a loose ball and was twisted around. When Marshall broke free, he started running the wrong way with the pigskin. Marshall's Viking teammates shouted for him to stop, but Marshall thought they were cheering him on. Jim Marshall rumbled 60-yards and carried the ball into his own end zone where he was brought down for a 2-point safety.

Gary "Big Hands" Johnson of the San Diego Chargers had 17½ quarterback sacks during the 1980 NFL season.

■

Defensive back Jack Tatum of the Oakland Raiders intercepted 30 passes during his nine year NFL career, but never returned an interception for a touchdown.

The Los Angeles Rams' defensive front four in the 1960's was made up of Merlin Olsen, Deacon Jones, Rosey Grier, and Lamar Lundy. Collectively those defensive linemen were known as "The Fearsome Foursome."

■

Linebacker Sam Mills starred at middle linebacker for the New Orleans Saints in the 1980's even though he was only 5 feet 9 inches tall and weighed only 225 pounds.

■

Randy Gradishar of the Denver Broncos returned an interception 93 yards for a touchdown against the Cleveland Browns on October 5, 1980.

■

Defensive tackle Warren Sapp of the Tampa Bay Buccaneers was a member of the 2002 All-NFL Defensive Team.

Defensive back Lester Hayes of the Oakland Raiders had 13 interceptions during the 1980 NFL season.

■

Derrick Thomas of the Kansas City Chiefs had seven QB sacks in one game against the Seattle Seahawks on November 11, 1990. He had six quarterback sacks in one game against the Oakland Raiders on September 6, 1998.

■

The most passes ever intercepted in a single NFL game by one player is four. It is a record shared by many players.

■

Linebacker Lawrence Taylor of the N.Y. Giants had 142 career quarterback sacks, counting his rookie stats in 1981. (Taylor was a rookie the year before QB sacks became an official NFL stat.)

In a 1969 sportwriters' poll, Gino Marchetti of the Baltimore Colts was voted the Best Defensive End in the NFL's first 50 years.

■

Franco Harris, a star running back for Penn State and the Pittsburgh Steelers, had brothers who both played defense at Penn State. Pete Harris played safety for the Nittany Lions and Guiseppe Harris played cornerback.

■

Linebacker Jack Lambert of the Pittsburgh Steelers had 28 interceptions in 11 NFL seasons.

■

Quarterback sacks became an official NFL stat in 1982.

DEFENSIVE COMEBACKS

William "The Fridge" Perry won fame in the NFL as a 6'2", 300 lb. defensive lineman. Perry weighed 305 pounds when he played nose tackle in college at Clemson. Someone once asked him about his size as a youngster. "When I was little, I was big," said Perry.

■

All-Pro defensive tackle Art Donovan always struggled to keep his weight down. Donovan once described his eating habits this way. "I was a light eater," said Art Donovan. "When it got light, I started to eat."

■

Defensive lineman Mike Reid of the Cincinnati Bengals said, "There are a thousand reasons for failure, but not a single excuse."

Middle linebacker Maxis Baugham of the Los Angeles Rams once described what it was like to call defenses for his team. "I'm the defensive quarterback," said Baugham.

■

Defensive lineman Buck Buchanan of the Kansas City Chiefs described the job of an NFL pass rusher this way. "You try to ring the quarterback's bell," said Buchanan.

■

Middle linebacker Nick Buoniconti of the Miami Dolphins summed up pro football this way. Buoniconti said, "Defense is the name of the game."

■

Football coach and former college linebacker Lou Holtz made this comment about bad breaks in a football game. "The man who complains about the way the ball bounces," said Lou Holtz, "is likely the one who dropped it."

In 1981, defensive end Willie Davis of the Green Bay
Packers became the first player from Grambling College
to be inducted into the Pro Football Hall of Fame.

■

Famous NFL coach Tom Landry of the Dallas Cowboys
was an All-Pro Defensive Back for the N.Y. Giants in
1954 and had 31 career interceptions.

■

All-Pro defensive tackle Bob Lilly of the Dallas
Cowboys played in 292 of a possible 293 games during
his NFL career.

Defensive tackle Dick Modzelewski, who played for several NFL teams, including the Washington Redskins and New York Giants, once started 180 consecutive NFL games.

■

Defensive end Doug Atkins, who is a member of the College and Pro Football Halls of Fame, went to the University of Tennessee on a basketball scholarship. Tennessee football coach Bob Neyland talked Atkins into going out for the gridiron squad.

■

In college, Herb Adderley was an offensive star at the University of Michigan. When Adderley went to play for the Green Bay Packers, he was converted into a defensive back.

■

Defensive back Herb Adderley of the Green Bay Packers and the Dallas Cowboys intercepted 48 passes during his NFL career and is a member of the Pro Football Hall of Fame.

Linebacker Ted Hendricks of the Baltimore Colts was nicknamed "The Mad Stork" because of his tall, thin frame.

■

Carl Mecklenburg of the Denver Broncos played defensive end, defensive tackle, and linebacker during his NFL career.

■

Defensive end Ed Jones of the Dallas Cowboys stood six feet nine inches tall and was nicknamed "Too Tall" Jones.

■

Star middle linebacker Harry Carson of the New York Giants played defensive end in college at South Carolina State.

■

Defensive end Andy Robustelli of the Los Angeles Rams and New York Giants played in the NFL from 1951 to 1964 and recovered 22 fumbles.

Middle linebacker Jack Reynolds of the Los Angeles Rams and San Francisco 49ers was nicknamed "Hacksaw." Jack "Hacksaw" Reynolds got his nickname because once in a fit of temper, he used a hacksaw to cut an old car into pieces.

■

Sports broadcaster Howie Long played defensive end at Villanova University and for the Los Angeles Raiders in the NFL.

■

Defensive tackle Leo Nomellini of the San Francisco 49ers was voted into the Pro Football Hall of Fame in 1969.

■

Linebacker Ray Nitschke of the Green Bay Packers was the MVP of the 1962 NFL Championship game when the Packers beat the New York Giants for the title.

Linebacker Mike Singletary of the Chicago Bears had 44 interceptions, 12 fumble recoveries and 19 quarterback sacks in his NFL career.

■

All-American middle linebacker Tommy Nobis of Texas was the first college player ever drafted by the Atlanta Falcons in the NFL draft. Nobis was picked in 1966, the Falcons' first year in the NFL.

CHAPTER 9

OFFENSIVE REMARKS

Quarterbacks get the newspaper headlines. Running backs and receivers get all the glory. Offensive linemen are the blue-collar gridiron guys who get the job done. Without them, there would be no offensive game. It's the center, guards, and tackles who put the offense in gear and make it go. They block! They knock down would-be tacklers! They open holes and protect the QB from mad pass rushers! Offensive linemen do much of the work and get little, if any, of the credit. So let's go O!

Chuck Bednarik of the Philadelphia Eagles was All-Pro at center in 1949 and 1950 and then All-Pro at linebacker from 1951 to 1956.

■

The "weak side" of an offensive line is the side where the split end lines up. It is called the weak side because it has only two blockers on that side of the center. The other side of the center is the "strong side" and has three blockers, including an offensive guard, an offensive tackle, and the tight end.

■

Offensive tackle, Bob Brown, who spent most of his NFL career with the Philadelphia Eagles, was elected to the Pro Football Hall of Fame in 2004.

■

The San Francisco 49ers made Kwame Harris, an offensive tackle from Stanford, their number one pick in the 2003 NFL draft.

NFL coach Forrest Gregg played offensive tackle for the Green Bay Packers under coach Vince Lombardi.

■

Famous football coach Glenn "Pop" Warner played guard at Cornell University.

■

Bill Warner, the younger brother of Glenn "Pop" Warner, also played guard at Cornell University and won All-America honors in 1901.

A "screen play" is a trick offensive play where defenders are purposely allowed to freely rush the quarterback as he retreats to pass. As the pass rush occurs, a receiver takes up a position near a wall of blockers assembled behind the line of scrimmage. The QB then softly tosses the ball over the heads of the charging defenders to the receiver.

■

An "option play" is an offensive play where the quarterback has the choice of handing off the ball, running with it himself, or passing it.

■

The Houston Texans averaged only 223.3 yards per game in total offense in 2003. It was the lowest offensive output of any NFL team that season.

■

Mike Webster of the Pittsburgh Steelers was named the center on the NFL's All-Time team, which was selected in 2000.

In pro football, an offensive team has 30 seconds to put the ball in play after the referee blows his whistle to signal: ready to play!

■

Offensive guard Reggie McKenzie of the Buffalo Bills was All-Pro his first two seasons after the Bills drafted him in 1972.

■

Center Mick Tingelhoff of the Minnesota Vikings was named All-Pro six consecutive years from 1964 to 1969. He played 240 consecutive games at center for the Minnesota Vikings during his NFL career.

■

A bootleg play in football is when a quarterback runs to the side opposite the direction most of his blockers are going. It is a play designed to confuse the defense.

Offensive tackle Jordan Gross of Utah was the number one pick of the Carolina Panthers in the 2003 NFL draft.

■

Center John Yarno was the first All-American football player in the University of Idaho's history. Yarno played in the NFL with the Seattle Seahawks.

■

The overtime rule for tied games in the NFL was established in 1974.

■

Guard Conrad Dobler of the New Orleans Saints, who had a reputation for extreme toughness, earned a degree in political science from the University of Wyoming.

■

The 2002 All-CFL team included offensive tackles Dave Mudge of the Winnipeg Blue Bombers and Uzooma Okeke of the Montreal Alouettes.

Three Wistert brothers were All-American tackles at the University of Michigan. Francis "Whitey" Wistert was an All-American tackle in 1933. Albert "Ox" Wistert was an All-American tackle in 1942. Alvin "Moose" Wistert was an All-American tackle in 1948 and 1949.

No offensive lineman has ever been named the MVP of the NFL or the AP Offensive Player of the Year.

Center Dave Rimington of Nebraska won the Outland Trophy as college football's top interior lineman in 1981 and 1982.

Tackle Rosie Brown was a Little All-American at Morgan State University in 1952 and All-Pro with the N.Y. Giants from 1956 to 1963.

■

Dick Wildung, an All-American offensive tackle at Minnesota in 1941 and 1942, was a P.T. boat skipper during World War II and later played pro football in the NFL with the Green Bay Packers.

■

Guard Joe DeLamielleure of the Buffalo Bills was elected to the Pro Football Hall of Fame in 2003.

■

The Carolina Panthers averaged only 267.5 yards per game in total offense in 2003, which was the lowest average in the NFC.

BLOCK HEADS QUIZ

Match each college football Hall of Fame lineman with the school he played for.

1. Frank J. Schwab (guard)
2. Hamilton Fish (tackle)
3. John McEwan (center)
4. Joseph Alexander (guard)
5. James Hogan (tackle)
6. Stanley Barnes (end)

A. California (1918-1921)
B. Yale (1902-1904)
C. Syracuse (1918-1920)
D. Army (1914-1916)
E. Harvard (1907-1909)
F. Lafayette (1919-1922)

The correct matches are:
1-F (Frank J. Schwab - Lafayette); 2-E (Hamilton Fish-Harvard); 3-D (John McEwan-Army); 4-C (Joseph Alexander-Syracuse); 5-B (James Hogan-Yale); and 6-A (Stanley Barnes-California).

Center Bryan Chiu of the Montreal Alouettes was voted the Most Outstanding Offensive Lineman in the Canadian Football League in 2002.

■

George Foster, an offensive tackle from Georgia, was the number one pick of the Denver Broncos in the 2003 NFL player draft.

■

In 2001, offensive tackle Bryant McKinnie of Miami won the Outland Trophy as the best college lineman in America.

■

All-American guard Jack Cannon of Notre Dame played college football in 1929 without wearing a helmet.

■

Roosevelt Brown and Anthony Munoz were voted the offensive tackles on the NFL's All-Time Team, which was selected in 2000.

Offensive tackle Ron Yary of USC was the NFL's number one draft pick in 1968. Yary was selected by the Minnesota Vikings.

■

Orlando Pace, an offensive tackle from Ohio State, was the first player taken in the 1997 NFL draft. Pace was picked by the St. Louis Rams.

■

Guard Ken Rice of Auburn was the only offensive lineman to be an overall number one pick in the AFL draft. Rice was the first player selected in the 1961 AFL draft and was picked by the Buffalo Bills.

■

Paul Bunker was Army's first All-American football player. Bunker was an All-American tackle in 1901.

Offensive tackle John Hicks of Ohio State won the Lombardi Trophy as college football's top lineman in 1973.

■

Pro Hall-of-Fame tackle Ron Mix, who played with the San Diego Chargers and Oakland Raiders, only had two holding penalties called against him during his ten-year NFL career.

CHAPTER 10

TAKE THAT BACK!

Take the handoff! Hit that hole! Run to daylight! Steamroll over some defenders, fake out a few others, and carry that pigskin to pay dirt in the end zone. These are the guys who grind out the yardage on the ground to score the tough touchdowns. They race for long gainers and take dangerous, headfirst dives over the goal line. These are the fast and famous bruising backs of football. Now is the time to meet them—head on!

Running back Archie Griffin of Ohio State was the first player to win the Heisman Trophy two times. Griffin captured college football's coveted prize in 1974 and in 1975.

■

Marcus Allen was the first running back from the Oakland/Los Angeles Raiders to win a league rushing title. Allen's 1,759 rushing yards in 1985 topped all AFC rushers.

■

Washington Redskins running back John Riggins led the NFC with 24 rushing touchdowns in 1983.

■

On September 29th, 2002, running back Shaun Alexander of the Seattle Seahawks scored five touchdowns in the first half of a NFL game against the Minnesota Vikings. Seattle won the game 48 to 23.

BARRY SANDERS TIDBITS

Barry Sanders was a five foot eight inch, 203 pound running back when the Detroit Lions made him their number one pick in the 1989 NFL draft.

■

The first time Barry Sanders of the Detroit Lions led the NFC in rushing was in 1989, his rookie season. Sanders rushed for 1,470 yards his first year as a pro.

■

Barry Sanders gained 15,269 yards rushing during his NFL career.

■

In 1997, Barry Sanders became the third back in NFL history to rush for over 2,000 yards a single season. Sanders gained 2,053 yards in 1997.

Running back Ron Dayne of Wisconsin won the Heisman Trophy in 1999.

■

In the New York Jets' 31 to 24 opening day victory over the Cincinnati Bengals in 2004, Jets' running back Curtis Martin rushed for 196 yards on 29 carries. It was one of the best opening day rushing performances in NFL history.

Dick Maegle of Rice rushed for 265 yards against Alabama in the 1954 Cotton Bowl which Rice won 28 to 6.

■

Herschel Walker won the NFC rushing title in 1988 when he gained 1,514 yards as a member of the Dallas Cowboys.

■

Alan Ameche was an All-American at Wisconsin in 1954 where he played fullback and linebacker.

■

Running back Nile Kinnick of the University of Iowa won the Heisman Trophy in 1939. Kinneck later became a Navy fighter pilot during WWII and died in a plane crash.

■

Halfback Joe Bellino of Navy won the Heisman Trophy in 1960.

WALTER PAYTON TIDBITS

Walter Payton of the Chicago Bears rushed for 16,726 yards during his 13-year NFL career and scored 110 rushing touchdowns. He lead the NFC in rushing from 1976 to 1980.

■

Running back Walter Payton stood 5 feet 10 inches tall and weighed 202 pounds.

■

Walter Payton scored a total of 125 touchdowns for the Chicago Bears as a rusher and receiver during his NFL career.

■

On November 20, 1977 Walter Payton rushed for 275 yards in a single game against the Minnesota Vikings to set a Chicago Bears' team record.

Charles White of USC rushed for 5,598 yards during his college career.

■

On opening day of the 1973 NFL season, O.J. Simpson of the Buffalo Bills rushed for 250 yards on 29 carries against the New England Patriots.

■

Jim Thorpe, one of the greatest running backs in the history of football, stood 6 feet 1 inch tall and weighed only 190 pounds.

■

Running back/flankerback Lenny Moore of the Baltimore Colts once scored touchdowns in 18 consecutive NFL games.

■

The winner of the Heisman Trophy in 1983 was running back Mike Rozier of Nebraska.

GALE SAYERS TIDBITS

Gale Sayers of the Chicago Bears scored a rushing touchdown, a receiving touchdown, and a touchdown returning a kick all in a single NFL game three different times during his NFL career.

■

Gale Sayers was an All-American running back at the University of Kansas and was nicknamed "The Kansas Comet."

■

Gale Sayers was named all-time NFL halfback in 1969 and All-NFL five years in a row.

Gale Sayers scored an NFL record six touchdowns in one game (vs. San Francisco) in 1965. That year he led the NFL in scoring (22 touchdowns).

■

During his NFL career, Gale Sayers of the Chicago Bears scored 39 rushing touchdowns, 9 receiving touchdowns, 2 touchdowns on punt returns and 6 touchdowns on kickoff returns. A knee injury cut short his amazing NFL career.

■

Gale Sayers is a member of the College and Pro Football Halls of Fame.

Eddie George of the Tennessee Oilers (now Titans) rushed for 216 yards on 35 carries against the Oakland Raiders on opening day of the 1997 NFL season.

■

Steve Stone was the first Notre Dame running back to gain 100 yards or more in a game four consecutive times. He did it in 1980.

■

In the Chicago Cardinals' 40 to 6 win over the Chicago Bears in 1929, fullback Ernie Nevers scored all of the Cardinals' 40 points.

In 1902, Neil Snow of Michigan scored five touchdowns against Stanford in the Rose Bowl, which Michigan won 49 to 0.

On opening day of the 1983 NFL season, George Rogers of the New Orleans Saints rushed for 206 yards on 24 carries against the St. Louis Cardinals.

■

Franco Harris of the Pittsburgh Steelers gained 1,055 yards rushing in 1972, his rookie season.

■

In 1962, Carlton "Cookie" Gilchrist of the Buffalo Bills became the first AFC running back to gain 1,000 yards in a single season. Gilchrist rushed for 1,096 yards in 1962.

■

Washington Redskins' runner Larry Brown, who twice led the NFC in rushing (1970 and 1972), was deaf in his left ear and wore a hearing aid to help him hear which plays were called.

JIM BROWN TIDBITS

Fullback Jim Brown of the Cleveland Browns was elected to the Pro Bowl nine consecutive times.

■

Jim Brown was an All-American in football and lacrosse at Syracuse University.

■

Jim Brown rushed for 12,312 yards and 106 touchdowns during his NFL career. He also caught 20 touchdown passes, for a career total of 126 touchdowns.

■

From 1957 to 1965, Jim Brown of the Cleveland Browns led the NFL in rushing every year except one.

■

In 1963, Jim Brown rushed for 1,863 yards on 291 carries for an average of 6.4 yards per carry.

Fullback Sam Francis of Nebraska was the number one pick of the second NFL draft, which was held in 1937. He was selected by the Philadelphia Eagles.

■

The Atlanta Falcons' Gerald Riggs rushed for 202 yards on 35 carries against the New Orleans Saints on opening day of the 1984 NFL season.

■

Joe "The Jet" Perry played for the San Francisco 49ers and the Baltimore Colts from 1957 to 1965 and rushed for a total of 8,378 yards.

Halfback Tom Harmon of Michigan was the first player selected in the 1941 NFL draft. He was picked by the Chicago Bears.

■

Tailback George Cafego of Tennessee was an All-American in 1939. Cafego was nicknamed "Bad News" because he always did things wrong in practice, but excelled in games.

■

Running back Duce Staley of the Philadelphia Eagles gained 201 yards in 26 carries against the Dallas Cowboys on opening day of the 2000 NFL season.

■

Willis McGahee of Miami and Larry Johnson of Penn State were the only running backs selected in the first round of the 2003 NFL draft. McGahee was picked by the Buffalo Bills and Johnson was selected by the Kansas City Chiefs.

The first Philadelphia Eagles' running back to gain 200 or more yards in a game was Steve Van Buren, who rushed for 205 yards against the Pittsburgh Steelers in 1949.

■

John Cappeletti started his college career as a defensive back at Penn State. As a junior, John Cappeletti was moved to running back, and as a senior he won the Heisman Trophy in 1973.

■

In 1979, Earl Campbell of the Houston Oilers won the Bert Bell Trophy as the NFL's Most Valuable Player. Campbell rushed for 1,697 yards and 19 touchdowns that season.

■

Tony Dorsett of the University of Pittsburgh rushed for 100 or more yards in a game 33 times during his college career.

TRUE BLUE RUNNING BACK QUIZ

Try your hand at figuring out whether these running back riddles are true or false.

1. True or false? Deuce McAllister of the New Orleans Saints gained more rushing yards than Tiki Barber of the N.Y. Giants during the 2002-2003 NFL season.

2. True or false? Marshall Faulk of San Diego State led the NCAA in rushing in 1991 and 1992.

3. True or false? A running back from Fordham University once won the NCAA rushing title.

Answers

1. True. Deuce McAllister led the NFC in rushing yards with 1,388 yards in 2002-2003. Tiki Barber gained 1,387 yards that same season.

2. True. Marshall Faulk led all college rushers in 1991 and 1992 with 1,429 yards and 1,630 yards.

3. True. In 1938, Len Eshmont of Fordham won the NCAA Rushing title with 831 yards.

From 2000 to 2003, running back Ahman Green of the Green Bay Packers rushed for 5,685 yards and scored 41 touchdowns.

■

Napoleon McCallum of Navy gained 7,172 all-purpose yards from 1981 to 1985.

■

Fullback Jim Taylor of the Green Bay Packers rushed for 1,474 yards in 1961 to capture the NFL rushing title.

■

Ken Simonton led the NFL Europe in rushing in the 2002-2003 season with a total of 871 yards.

■

Running back George Rogers of South Carolina rushed for over 100 yards in every one of his 11 regular season college games in 1980.

John "Frenchy" Fuqua of the Pittsburgh Steelers gained 218 yards rushing and scored two touchdowns against the Philadelphia Eagles on December 20, 1970.

■

In 1999, LaDainian Tomlinson of Texas Christian University rushed for 406 yards against the University of Texas-El Paso (UTEP).

■

Running back John Avery of the Edmonton Eskimos led the CFL in rushing during the 2002 season with 1,448 yards.

■

Earl Campbell of the Houston Oilers rushed for 200 yards or more in a single game four times during the 1980 NFL season.

Calvin Hill of the Dallas Cowboys rushed for 1,036 yards in 1972 and gained 1,142 yards in 1973. Fullback Jim Nance of the Boston Patriots won the AFL rushing titles in 1966 and 1967. Nance gained 1,458 yards in 1966 and 1,216 yards in 1967.

■

Leroy Kelly of the Cleveland Browns scored 74 touchdowns during his NFL career which lasted from 1964 to 1973.

■

Bo Jackson of the Oakland Raiders gained 221 yards against the Seattle Seahawks on November 30, 1987.

■

Doug Russell of the Chicago Cardinals led the NFL in rushing in 1935 by gaining only 499 yards.

EMMITT SMITH TIDBITS

Emmitt Smith played college football at the University of Florida, where he was an All-American running back.

■

As a Dallas Cowboy, Emmitt Smith led the NFC in rushing three consecutive times from 1991 to 1993. He also led the NFC in rushing in 1995.

■

In 1995, Emmitt Smith tallied 25 touchdowns and led the NFC in scoring with 150 points.

■

Emmitt Smith rushed for over 17,000 yards in his NFL career.

■

Emmitt Smith retired from the NFL in February of 2005.

Edgerrin James of the Indianapolis Colts won his first AFC rushing title in 1999 when he gained 1,553 yards on 369 carries.

■

Cornell's Ed Marinaro gained 4,715 yards in his college career.

■

In 1973, O.J. Simpson of the Buffalo Bills rushed for 100 or more yards in a single NFL game 11 times.

■

Running back Floyd Little of Syracuse rushed for 216 yards against Tennessee in the 1966 Gator Bowl, which was won by Tennessee 18 to 12.

■

Ron Johnson gained 1,182 yards while playing running back for the N.Y. Giants in 1972.

■

In September of 1990, Thurman Thomas of the Buffalo Bills gained 214 yards on 18 carries against the N.Y. Jets.

CHAPTER 11

SPECIAL GUYS

These are the players who get a real kick out of football. They boot field goals. They punt. They handle kickoffs. These are also the speedy return guys who field those kicks. They are all special in their own unique ways. We hope you too get a kick from reading about these special football stars.

Jim Bakken of the St. Louis Cardinals kicked seven field goals in one game against the Pittsburgh Steelers on September 24, 1967.

When the AFC beat the NFC 15 to 13 in the 1974 NFL Pro Bowl, place-kicker Garo Yepremian of the Miami Dolphins was named the MVP of the game.

■

Charlie Gogolak of the Washington Redskins kicked nine P.A.T.'s (Points After Touchdowns) against the N.Y. Giants on November 27, 1966.

■

Gino Cappelletti of the Boston Patriots (now New England) led the American Football League in scoring five times. He was the AFL's top scorer in 1961 and from 1963 to 1966. Cappelletti's best year was in 1964 when he scored seven touchdowns, kicked 25 field goals, and booted 38 points after touchdowns for a total of 155 points.

Kicker Mike Prindle of Western Michigan kicked 7 field goals in a 42–7 win over college rival Marshall on September 29, 1984.

■

Roman Anderson of Houston kicked 70 field goals and 213 P.A.T's for a total of 423 points during his college career, which lasted from 1988 to 1991.

■

Adam Vinatieri of the New England Patriots was the kicker selected to the 2002 All-NFL team.

■

In 1998, Gary Anderson of the Minnesota Vikings made 35 or 35 attempted field goals during the NFL season.

In 1950, Doak Walker of the Detroit Lions led the NFL in scoring as a rookie with 128 points. Walker scored 11 touchdowns and booted 8 field goals and 38 P.A.T's that season.

■

In 1953, Lou "The Toe" Groza of the Cleveland Browns became the first player in NFL history to kick more than 20 field goals in a single season. Groza kicked 23 field goals that year

■

Gene Mingo of the Denver Broncos led the AFL in scoring during its first year of operation. In 1960, as a rookie Mingo scored six touchdowns, kicked 18 field goals, and booted 33 P.A.T.'s for a total of 123 points.

PAUL HORNUNG TIDBITS

Green Bay Packers' star Paul Hornung led the NFL in scoring in 1959, 1960, and 1961.

■

In 1959, Paul Hornung scored 7 T.D.'s, kicked 7 field goals, and booted 31 P.A.T.'s to lead the NFL with 94 points.

■

In 1960, Paul Hornung led the NFL in scoring when he kicked 15 field goals, scored 15 T.D.'s, and booted 41 P.A.T.'s for a total of 176 points.

■

In 1961, Paul Hornung scored 10 touchdowns, booted 15 field goals, and kicked 41 P.A.T.'s for 146 points.

Kicker Jay Feely of the Atlanta Falcons led the NFC in scoring in 2002 with 32 field goals and 42 P.A.T's for a total of 138 points.

■

Jason Elam of the Denver Broncos kicked a 63-yard field goal against the Jacksonville Jaguars on October 25, 1998.

■

Kicker Jim Turner of the New York Jets led the AFC in scoring in 1968 with 145 points and in 1969 with 129 points.

■

John Lee, a kicker for UCLA, booted 29 field goals during the 1984 season.

■

Jeff Jaeger of the University of Washington kicked 80 field goals in his college career, which lasted from 1983 to 1986.

The Washington Redskins' Chip Lohmiller led the NFC in scoring in 1991 with 149 points.

■

In 1977, Steve Little of Arkansas and Russell Erxleben of Texas both booted 67-yard field goals in college football games. Little kicked a 67-yard field goal against Texas while Erxleben kicked a 67-yard field goal against Rice.

■

Gale Sayers of the Chicago Bears is the NFL's all-time leading kick-return specialist. During his NFL career, Sayers returned 338 kickoffs for 2,781 yards, which is an average of 30.6 yards per return.

■

Bill Blackstock of Tennessee averaged 25.9 yards per punt return in 1951.

Paul Allen of BYU averaged 40.1 yards per kickoff return in 1961.

■

Santana Moss of the N.Y. Jets was selected as the punt return specialist on the 2002 All-NFL Team.

■

In 1958, Ollie Matson of the Chicago Cardinals averaged 35.5 yards per kickoff return.

■

Bob Hayes of the Dallas Cowboys averaged 20.8 yards per punt return in 1968.

■

Noland Smith of the Kansas City Chiefs returned a kickoff 106 yards for a touchdown against the Denver Broncos on December 17, 1967.

In 1967, Travis Williams of the Green Bay Packers averaged 41.1 yards per kickoff return.

■

George McAfee of the Chicago Bears returned 112 punts for 1,431 yards during his 8-year NFL career.

■

Herb Rich of the Baltimore Colts averaged 23.0 yards per punt return in 1950.

Nick Murphy of the Barcelona Dragons was the punter on the 2002-03 All-NFL Europe team.

■

Yale Lary of the Detroit Lions punted 503 times during his 11-year NFL career for 22,279 yards and a 44.3 yards per punt average.

■

Sammy Baugh of the Washington Redskins is the all-time leading punter in the NFL. Baugh booted 338 punts during his 16-year career for 15,245 yards and an average of 45.1 yards per punt.

CHAPTER 12

TEAM SPIRIT

It is sometimes difficult to explain what separates a great team from a good team. Many coaches believe a good team has some great individual players, but a great team has many good players who all work well together. Whatever the case, all the gridiron squads you'll read about on the following pages are winning teams in their own ways.

The New York Giants were founded by Tim Mara in 1925 and joined the NFL that year for an expansion fee of $2,500.

■

The New York Giants won their first NFL Championship in 1927 with a record of 11 wins, 1 loss, and 1 tie.

■

The Atlanta Falcons joined the NFL as an expansion team in 1966 for a franchise fee of $8,500,000.

■

In 1966, the Atlanta Falcons won their first NFL game ever by defeating the N.Y. Giants 27 to 16.

Cecil Isbell, a former NFL quarterback for the Green Bay Packers, was the first head coach of the Baltimore Colts.

■

In 1984, the Baltimore Colts moved to Indianapolis and became the Indianapolis Colts.

■

The Chicago Bears were once nicknamed the "Monsters of the Midway" because they liked to punish their opponents on the gridiron.

■

George Halas coached Chicago to NFL Championships in 1921, 1933, 1934, 1937, 1940, 1946, and 1947.

■

The Cleveland Browns scored 423 points during the 1946 season while holding their opponents to a total of only 137 points.

The Cleveland Browns were the first pro team to hire their coaching staff all year round.

■

Paul Brown of the Cleveland Browns was one of the first football coaches to use playbooks and to develop game plans.

Tom Landry coached the Dallas Cowboys from 1960 to 1988 and won 270 games.

■

Hall-of-Fame quarterback Sammy Baugh was the head coach of the New York Titans in 1960.

■

The New England Patriots established a NFL record in 2004 by winning 21 consecutive football games over the course of two NFL seasons. The record-winning streak came to an end on October 31, 2004 when the Pittsburgh Steelers defeated the New England Patriots by the score of 34 to 20.

■

The team colors of the New England Patriots are blue, red, silver, and white.

When the New York Titans were renamed the New York Jets in 1963, the quarterbacks on the team were Galen Hall, Dick Wood, and John Green.

■

In 1971, John Mazur was the head coach of the Patriots team when the Boston Patriots were renamed the New England Patriots.

■

In 1930, the Portsmouth (Ohio) Spartans joined the National Football League. In 1934, the Portsmouth Spartans moved to Detroit and became the Detroit Lions.

■

The Dallas Cowboys beat the Pittsburgh Steelers 27 to 24 in 1961 to record the Cowboys' very first NFL victory.

The Cleveland Browns joined the NFL in 1937.
The team became the Los Angeles Rams in 1946.

■

The Los Angeles Rams won the NFC Championship
in 1979.

■

The Los Angeles Rams became the St. Louis Rams
in 1995.

■

The Minnesota Vikings first year as a NFL team
was in 1961 when their head coach was NFL
Hall-of-Famer Norm Van Brocklin.

■

Bud Grant won 168 NFL games as the head coach
of the Minnesota Vikings.

■

The Jacksonville Jaguars team colors are teal, black,
and gold.

Tom Coughlin was the first head coach of the Jacksonville Jaguars.

■

Dom Capers was the first head coach of the Carolina Panthers.

■

In 1996, the original Cleveland Browns moved to Baltimore and became the Baltimore Ravens.

■

The Baltimore Ravens coached by Brian Billick won the AFC championship in 2000.

■

The New Orleans Saints team colors are gold, black, and white.

QB Jim Everett of the New Orleans Saints passed for 3,970 yards during the 1995 NFL season.

■

The Buffalo Bills were an original member of the American Football League and became part of the NFL in 1970.

O.J. Simpson of USC was named the number one pick in the 1969 NFL draft when he was selected by the Buffalo Bills.

■

The first man to coach the Cincinnati Bengals was football innovator Paul Brown. Brown assumed the gridiron reigns of the Bengals when Cincinnati joined the NFL in 1968.

■

The team colors of the Cincinnati Bengals are black, orange, and white.

■

The first head coach of the Denver Broncos was Frank Filchock, who guided the team in 1960.

■

When the Denver Broncos first became a member team of the NFL in 1970, the Broncos won only 5 of 14 games (1 tie).

The Houston Oilers became the Tennessee Oilers in 1997. In 1999, the Tennessee Oilers were renamed the Tennessee Titans.

■

The Philadelphia Eagles were originally the NFL franchise known as the Frankford Yellow Jackets.

■

Coach Earle "Greasy" Neale was the man who introduced the Philadelphia Eagles to football's T-formation.

■

The Philadelphia Eagles played their first NFL game in 1933.

In 1933, Art Rooney bought an NFL franchise for $2,500 which became the Pittsburgh Steelers team.

■

The first coach of the Pittsburgh Steelers was player/coach Johnny Blood, whose real name was John McNally. McNally played football under a pseudonym during his entire pro career.

■

In 1952, the San Francisco 49ers NFL franchise was in serious financial trouble until the team signed college star Hugh McElhenny to a contract. McElhenny was so popular with football fans he filled the stands for San Francisco's games and helped save the franchise.

■

The San Francisco 49ers played their first NFL games in 1950. The 49ers won three games and lost nine that year.

The Tampa Bay Buccaneers were 0-14 their first year in the National Football League, which was 1976.

■

In 2004, the Tampa Bay Buccaneers had two QB's on their team who were both sons of former Super-Bowl-champion quarterbacks. The Bucs' Chris Simms is the son of Phil Simms (Giants) and Brian Griese is the son of Bob Griese (Dolphins).

■

The Tampa Bay Buccaneers won the NFC championship in 2002 by defeating the Philadelphia Eagles 27 to 10 in the title contest.

■

In 1932, the Boston Braves became a NFL team. The Braves were renamed the Redskins in 1933. In 1937, the Redskins moved to Washington and became the Washington Redskins.

William "Lone Star" Dietz, a Native American, was the coach of the (Boston) Washington Redskins from 1933 and 1934.

■

The team colors of the Kansas City Chiefs are red, gold, and white.

■

The Arizona Cardinals are one of the NFL's oldest teams. The Cardinals were members of the American Professional Football Association in 1920 (APFA became the NFL).

■

The Arizona Cardinals were originally the Chicago Cardinals. In 1960, the Cardinals became the St. Louis Cardinals. In 1988, the Cardinals moved to Phoenix (Arizona), and in 1994 the team was renamed the Arizona Cardinals.

The Miami Dolphins joined the American Football League in 1966 and became part of the NFL when the AFL and NFL merged in 1970.

■

In 1972, the Miami Dolphins posted a perfect record of 16 wins and 0 losses, including a Super Bowl victory.

■

From 1971 to 1973, the Miami Dolphins, guided by coach Don Shula, won 40 games, lost 7, and tied 1 game.

■

The San Diego Chargers' franchise was owned by Barron Hilton, the son of hotel tycoon Conrad Hilton, until 1966.

Sid Gillman was the San Diego Chargers' first head coach. Gillman won a total of 90 games with the Chargers.

■

The team colors of the Seattle Seahawks are blue, green, and silver.

■

The Seattle Seahawks' first year in the NFL was in 1976.

■

The head coach of the Seattle Seahawks from 1976 to 1982 was Jack Patera.

■

Al Davis was the head coach of the Oakland Raiders from 1963 to 1965 and posted a career record of 23 wins, 16 losses, and 3 ties.

NICKNAME GAME

Can you correctly match each of the following Division 1-AA football schools with its team nickname?

1. Richmond
2. Morehead State
3. Princeton
4. Morgan State
5. Furman
6. Bucknell

A. Eagles
B. Bears
C. Tigers
D. Spiders
E. Bisons
F. Paladins

The correct matches are 1-D (Richmond Spiders); 2-A (Morehead State Eagles); 3-C (Princeton Tigers); 4-B (Morgan State Bears); 5-F (Furman Paladins); and 6-E (Bucknell Bisons).

John Madden, the Oakland Raiders' most famous head coach, was drafted by the Philadelphia Eagles as a tackle in 1959. A knee injury suffered in training camp ended John Madden's playing career.

■

John Madden was an assistant coach with the Oakland Raiders in 1967 and 1968. In 1969, John Madden became the head coach of the Oakland Raiders and guided the team to a season record of 12 wins, 1 loss, and 1 tie.

■

The Oakland Raiders lost to the Kansas City Chiefs in the 1969 AFL title game by the score of 17 to 7.

■

In 1908, Washington and Jefferson College became the first school to put numbers on the jerseys of its football players.

The nickname of the Iowa State football team is the "Cyclones" and its team colors are cardinal and gold.

■

Middle Tennessee State beat Idaho 70 to 58 on October 6, 2001. In the contest, the teams' combined for a total of 1,445 total yards.

■

Ara Parseghian compiled a career record of 95 wins, 17 losses, and 4 ties in 11 seasons as the head coach of Notre Dame. In 1980, Parseghian was voted into the College Football Hall of Fame.

■

The first Army-Navy football clash was played in 1890. Navy won the game beating Army 24 to 0. Army topped Navy the following year by a score of 32 to 16.

NICKNAME GAME #2

Can you correctly match each of the following Division 1-A football schools with its team nickname?

1. Vanderbilt
2. Louisville
3. Miami-Ohio
4. Arizona State
5. Idaho
6. Temple

A. Red Hawks
B. Commodores
C. Cardinals
D. Sun Devils
E. Owls
F. Vandals

The correct matches are 1-B (Vanderbilt Commodores); 2-C (Louisville Cardinals); 3-A (Miami-Ohio Red Hawks); 4-D (Arizona State Sun Devils); 5-F (Idaho Vandals); and 6-E (Temple Owls).

Jim Thorpe once called Harvard's Ed Mahan "The greatest back in football." Mahan was an All-American back at Harvard in 1913, 1914, and 1915.

■

The University of Washington went 63 games without a gridiron loss from 1907 to 1917. Washington's overall record during that streak was 59 wins and 4 ties.

■

The Associated Press declared the University of Maryland the national champions of college football in 1953.

■

In 13 years as the head football coach at Boston College and then Notre Dame, Frank Leahy won 107 games, lost only 13, and tied 9.

Columbia University once lost 44 football games in a row. In 1988, the Columbia Lions beat the Princeton Tigers 16 to 14 to end the losing streak.

■

The Miami Hurricanes won 29 football games in a row from 1990 to 1993.

■

Prairie View A & M lost 80 straight college football games from 1989 to 1998. On September 26, 1998, Prairie View A & M beat Langston 14 to 12 to end the losing streak.

■

Montana beat Furman 13 to 7 to win college football's Division 1-AA National Championship in 2001.

■

The nickname of the Rutgers University football team is the Scarlet Knights.

YALE UNIVERSITY UNBEATEN STREAKS

Yale University has had more unbeaten streaks in college football than any other team. Consider the following:

Yale footballers won 42 games and tied 5 games from 1879 to 1885.

■

From 1885 to 1889, Yale University won 47 football games and tied one game.

■

Yale won 37 consecutive college football games from 1890 to 1893.

■

Yale won 42 college gridiron contests and tied two from 1894 to 1896.

The University of Texas won the Southwest Football
Conference Championship from 1969 to 1973.

■

On October 9, 2004 Notre Dame won its 800th
college football game when it defeated Stanford
23 to 15.

■

Holy Cross has won over 550 college football games.

■

The National Championship Foundation declared
Lafayette College the National Champions of
College Football in 1896. Lafayette posted a
gridiron record of 11-0-1 that year.

CHAPTER 13

THE FINAL WHISTLE

Tweet! Time is running out, football fans. It's time for the two minute drill. Take a minute or two and see if you knew that the celebrities on the following pages all had past or present connections to the sport of football.

Former NFL quarterback John Elway is the owner of an Arena football team.

■

Rock star Jon Bon Jovi is the owner of an Arena football team.

Actor and pro wrestler "The Rock," whose real name is Dwayne Johnson, played defensive end at the University of Miami.

■

Dwayne "The Rock" Johnson played pro football in Canada for the Calgary Stampeders.

■

Television star Dean Cain, who played Superman on TV, played college football at Princeton University. He had a NFL tryout with the Buffalo Bills, but a knee injury ended his football career.

■

Minnesota Vikings running back Ed Marinaro was a co-star on the T.V. shows *Laverne & Shirley* and *Hill Street Blues*.

■

Movie star Mark Harmon played college football at UCLA.

Movie star Meryl Streep was a football cheerleader at Bernards High School in New Jersey.

■

The sports movie *Rudy* is based on the true story of a Notre Dame football player.

■

The sports movie *Remember the Titans* is based on the true story of a high school football team.

■

Defensive end Fred Dryer of the Los Angeles Rams played a detective on the T.V. show *Hunter*.

Defensive tackle Alex Karras of the Detroit Lions was a co-star on the T.V. show *Webster*.

■

Before he became a movie star, John Wayne was a football player at the University of Southern California.

■

African-American actor Woody Strode, who appeared in more than 60 films, including *Spartacus* and *The Ten Commandments*, played college football at UCLA and pro football for the Los Angeles Rams.

■

Burt Lancaster played the title role of Jim Thorpe in the movie *Jim Thorpe All American*.

■

NFL Hall of Fame running back Jim Brown co-starred in many movies, including *The Dirty Dozen* with Lee Marvin.

Monday Night Football first appeared on television in 1970.

■

The original *Monday Night Football* broadcast crew included Keith Jackson, Howard Cosell, and "Dandy" Don Meredith, a former quarterback for the Dallas Cowboys.

■

Professional football was first seen on national television in 1956.

■

Football sportscaster Pat Summerall's real first name is George.

■

On December 20, 1980, the N.Y. Jets and Miami Dolphins football game was televised without using any announcers. The Jets quietly won the game, beating the Dolphins 24 to 17.

Actor Ed Harris played football at Columbia University.

■

Carl Weathers, who co-starred in the first *Rocky* movies, played pro football for the Oakland Raiders.

SOME GUYS TALKING SPORTS

Comic Bill Cosby:
We lost every week. We lost to schools I never heard of. I think guys used to get together and invent a name so they could play us. One year we lost to a school called 'we want u'."

■

Comedian Rodney Dangerfield:
"Our school was so tough that in our football games after they sacked the quarterback, they went after his family."

■

Sportscaster Frank Gifford:
"Pro football in like nuclear warfare. There are no winners, only survivors."

Sports and comedy writer M.J. Pellowski:
"Fifty percent of the game of football is mental, so use your brains. Unfortunately, the other fifty percent of the game someone spends trying to knock those brains out."

■

Football coach Walt Michaels:
"Everyone has some fear. A man who has no fear belongs in a mental institution . . . or on special teams."

■

Charles Conerly, veteran NFL quarterback:
"When you win, you're an old pro. When you lose, you're an old man."

Actor Owen Wilson broke his nose playing football in high school.

■

Famous film director Terrence Malik played high school football in Texas.

■

Mr. T, whose real name is Lawrence Tureaud, played football in high school.

■

Comic and actor Jamie Foxx played quarterback for his high school football team.

■

Jesse James, the famous car and motorcycle designer, played high school football.

Snoop Dogg played high school football and has coached his son's youth football team.

Actor Kevin Costner played football in high school.

■

All-American end Paul Robeson of Rutgers became a Broadway star and an internationally famous singer. He starred in *Porgy and Bess*, *Showboat*, *and The Emperor Jones*.

■

NFL Hall-of-Fame tackle Merlin Olsen was a co-star on the T.V. show *Little House on the Prairie*.

■

Defensive end Bubba Smith of the Baltimore Colts appeared in the *Police Academy* movies.

Defensive tackle Otis Sistrunk of the Oakland Raiders appeared in the movie *Car Wash*.

■

Actor James Caan played college football at Michigan State University.

■

The famous T.V. movie *Brian's Song* is about the friendship and playing careers of Chicago Bears' running backs Brian Piccolo and Gale Sayers. Tragically, Brian Piccolo died of cancer early in his career. James Cann played Brian Piccolo and Billy Dee Williams played Gale Sayers.

■

The movie *The Longest Yard*, starring Burt Reynolds, featured former NFL stars Joe Kapp, Sonny Sixkiller, and Ray Nitschke.

Actor Burt Reynolds attended Florida State University on a football scholarship. An injury ended Reynolds' football career.

■

The movie *North Dallas Forty*, starring Nick Nolte, is based on the novel written by former Dallas Cowboys' wide receiver Peter Gent.

■

Fred "The Hammer" Williamson, who played for the Kansas City Chiefs as a cornerback, became an action star in Hollywood movies.

■

NBA star Grant Hill is the son of the NFL star Calvin Hill.

In the movie *Any Given Sunday*, former New York Giants' linebacker Lawrence Taylor played a football player, and Hall-of-Famer Jim Brown played a defensive coach for a fictitious NFL team. Other NFL players who appear in the movie include Terrell Owens, Irving Fryar, and Ricky Walters.

■

Heavyweight boxer Ken Norton's son, Ken Norton, Jr., played linebacker in the NFL.

■

About 150,000 youngsters play high school football in Texas each year.

■

NFL lineman Rosey Grier appeared as a co-star on the *Daniel Boone* T.V. show.

■

In 1998, *People Magazine* named Kansas City quarterback Elvis Grbac its sexiest athlete of the year.

Comedian John Candy was once part owner of the CFL's Toronto Argonauts.

■

Cole Porter wrote "The Bulldog Fight Song" for Yale University.

PIGSKIN POLITICS

President Ronald Reagan broadcast the football games of the University of Iowa on the radio in the early 1930's.

■

Actor Ronald Reagan played Notre Dame All-American George Gipp in the movie, *The Knute Rockne Story*.

■

Quarterback Jack Kemp of the Buffalo Bills retired from pro football and became a U.S. congressman.

Prior to being elected President, Woodrow Wilson served as a football faculty advisor at Wesleyan College.

■

Herbert Hoover (America's 31st President) helped organize the football squad at Stanford in 1891 and was a team manager.

■

Franklin D. Roosevelt (32nd president) played on Harvard's freshman football team in 1900 and was elected captain.

■

John F. Kennedy (35th president) played end at Harvard on the freshman team in 1936 and on the J.V. team in 1937.

Dwight D. Eisenhower (34th president) was a starting halfback on the West Point football team in 1912. Eisenhower once played in a game against Jim Thorpe.

■

Richard Nixon (37th president) was a reserve quarterback on the Whittier College football team in the 1930's.

■

Gerald Ford (38th president) was a star offensive center for the University of Michigan football team which went undefeated in 1932 and 1933.

■

Gerald Ford was voted the MVP of the 1934 Michigan football team.

The NFL's Green Bay Packers offered Gerald Ford a pro football tryout, but he declined in order to go into politics.

■

Byron "Whizzer" White, an All-American halfback at the University of Colorado, became an associate justice of the Supreme Court in 1962.

FINAL WINNING WORDS

"One man practicing sportsmanship is far better than a hundred teaching it."

Notre Dame football coach Knute Rockne.

■

"Winning is not everything—but making the effort to win is."

Green Bay Packers' coach Vince Lombardi

■

"When the one great scorer comes to write against your name, He marks—not that you won or lost—but how you played the game."

Sportswriter Grantland Rice

INDEX

ABOUT THE AUTHOR

Michael J. Pellowski won numerous all-star awards as a New Jersey high school football player during the 1960's and attended Rutgers University on a full athletic scholarship. At Rutgers, he started every game of his college career as a defensive end. He played in college football's 100th anniversary game in 1969. Pellowski was defensive captain of the 1970 Rutgers gridiron squad and won ECAC and AP All-East Division 1 honors. His 17-career quarterback sacks still rank among the top ten all-time leaders in that category at Rutgers.

After college, Pellowski had professional football trials in the NFL with the New England Patriots and in the Canadian Football League with the Montreal Alouettes. He played several years of semi-pro football, including a year with the Hartford Knights of the ACFL. Mr. Pellowski also coached high school football and has penned many books.

If you liked this book, you'll love all this series:

Little Giant® Book of "True" Ghost Stories • Little Giant® Book of "True" Ghostly Tales • Little Giant® Book of After School Fun • Little Giant® Book of Amazing Mazes • Little Giant® Book of Animal Facts • Little Giant® Book of Basketball • Little Giant® Book of Brain Twisters • Little Giant® Book of Card Games • Little Giant® Book of Card Tricks • Little Giant® Book of Cool Optical Illusions • Little Giant® Book of Dinosaurs • Little Giant® Book of Dominoes • Little Giant® Book of Eerie Thrills & Unspeakable Chills • Little Giant® Book of Giggles • Little Giant® Book of Football Facts • Little Giant® Book of Insults & Putdowns • Little Giant® Book of Jokes • Little Giant® Book of Kids' Games • Little Giant® Book of Knock-Knocks • Little Giant® Book of Laughs • Little Giant® Book of Magic Tricks • Little Giant® Book of Math Puzzles • Little Giant® Book of Mini-Mysteries • Little Giant® Book of Optical Illusion Fun • Little Giant® Book of Optical Illusions • Little Giant® Book of Optical Tricks • Little Giant® Book of Riddles • Little Giant® Book of School Jokes • Little Giant® Book of Science Experiments • Little Giant® Book of Science Facts • Little Giant® Book of Side-Splitters • Little Giant® Book of Tongue Twisters • Little Giant® Book of Travel Fun • Little Giant® Book of Travel Games • Little Giant® Book of Tricks & Pranks • Little Giant® Book of Visual Tricks • Little Giant® Book of Weird & Wacky Facts • Little Giant® Book of Whodunits

Available at fine stores everywhere.